RICHARD SEYMOUR lives, works and writes in London. He runs the Lenin's Tomb website, which casts a critical eye on the War on Terror, Islamophobia and neoliberalism. He is the author of *The Meaning of David Cameron*, *The Liberal Defence of Murder*, and *American Insurgents: A Brief History of American Anti-Imperialism*.

COUNTERBLASTS

COUNTERBLASTS is a series of short, polemical titles that aims to revive a tradition inaugurated by Puritan and Leveller pamphleteers in the seventeenth century, when, in the words of one of their number, Gerard Winstanley, the old world was 'running up like parchment in the fire'. From 1640 to 1663, a leading bookseller and publisher, George Thomason, recorded that his collection alone contained over twenty thousand pamphlets. Such polemics reappeared both before and during the French, Russian, Chinese, and Cuban revolutions of the last century.

In a period where politicians, media barons, and their ideological hirelings rarely challenge the basis of existing society, it is time to revive the tradition. Verso's Counterblasts will challenge the apologists of Empire and Capital.

Unhitched: The Trial of Christopher Hitchens

Richard Seymour

VERSO
London • New York

First published by Verso 2012
© Richard Seymour 2012

1 3 5 7 9 10 8 6 4 2

Verso
UK: 6 Meard Street, London W1F 0EG
US: 20 Jay Street, Suite 1010, Brooklyn, NY 11201
www.versobooks.com

Verso is the imprint of New Left Books

ISBN-13 978-1-84467-990-4

British Library Cataloguing in Publication Data
A catalogue record for this book is available from the British Library

Library of Congress Cataloging-in-Publication Data
Seymour, Richard, 1977-
 Unhitched : the trial of Christopher Hitchens / Richard Seymour. – 1st edition.
    pages cm. – (Counterblasts)
 Includes bibliographical references.
 ISBN 978-1-84467-990-4 (paperback : alkaline paper) –
ISBN (invalid) 978-1-84467-991-1 (ebook)
1. Hitchens, Christopher. 2. Hitchens, Christopher – Political and social views.
3. Right and left (Political science) – United States. 4. Intellectuals – United States –
Biography. 5. Journalists – United States – Biography. 6. Political activists –
United States – Biography. 7. British Americans – Biography. I. Title.
 CT275.H62575S49 2012
 320.092 – dc23
 [B]
                                2012039467

Typeset in Minion Pro by MJ Gavan, Truro, Cornwall
Printed in the US by Maple Vail

To Marie, whose hatred is pure. With all my love.

CONTENTS

PROLOGUE: PREDICTABLE AS HELL

I have never been able, except in my lazier moments, to employ the word predictable as a term of abuse … Speaking purely for myself, I should be alarmed if my knee failed to respond to certain stimuli. It would warn me of a loss of nerve … In the charmed circle of neoliberal and neoconservative journalism, however, 'unpredictability' is the special emblem and certificate of self-congratulation. To be able to bray that 'as a liberal, I say bomb the shit out of them' is to have achieved that eye-catching, versatile marketability that is so beloved of editors and talk-show hosts. As a life-long socialist, I say don't let's bomb the shit out of them. See what I mean? It lacks the sex appeal, somehow. Predictable as hell.

– Christopher Hitchens, 'Blunt Instruments'

If you're actually certain that you're hitting only a concentration of enemy troops [with cluster bombs] … then it's pretty good because those steel pellets will go straight through somebody and out the other side and through somebody else. And if they're bearing a Koran over their heart, it'll go straight through that, too. So they won't be able to say, 'Ah, I was bearing a Koran over my heart and guess what, the missile stopped halfway through.' No way, 'cause it'll go straight through that as well. They'll be dead, in other words.

– Christopher Hitchens to Adam Shatz in the *Nation*

In his benediction for Christopher Hitchens, who had just died from oesophageal cancer, the former British Prime Minister Tony Blair averred: 'He was a complete one-off in a world full of very stereotypical people, he was deeply unusual … He was also a thoroughly decent person and if he thought a cause was right, took it up even if it wasn't popular, even if it brought him a certain amount of criticism.'[1] In many ways Hitchens *was* a one-off. The sum of the attitudes and dispositions he carried with him to the grave made him idiosyncratic rather than simply tendentious. Among the usually forgettable ranks of ex-leftists, Hitchens stood out as one determined to stand out. There have been two well-trodden routes out of the left for those who want to leave it. The first is to gravitate towards a version of what Mark Fisher has called 'capitalist realism' – in the US context this would mean supporting the Democratic Party and the centre-right consensus.[2] The second is to swerve rapidly to the hard right, à la David Horowitz, and reject one's past commitments as a destructive error of youth. Hitchens rejected both paths, defending his quondam radicalism even as he embraced imperialism and American nationalism. He identified with no tendency, other than his own idiosyncrasy, a mugwump who occasionally masqueraded as a Marxist. The literary critic Terry Eagleton partially captures the strangeness of this brew: 'In some ways, Hitchens is a reactionary English patrician, in other ways a closet Thatcherite, and in yet other ways a right-leaning liberal.'[3]

None of this was entirely novel for Hitchens, who always made a virtue of his contradictory stances. Hitchens's story was, then, not exactly that of a noble mind overthrown, even if there was some form of regime change after the Twin Towers collapsed. Rather, the elements of his peculiar political personality were displaced, shaken up by events, and recomposed in a new articulation that leaned heavily to the right. Where once his career-minded avarice and desire for recognition from the rich and powerful coexisted with socialist commitment (hence the affectionate nickname 'Hypocritchens' that he acquired at Oxford), his ambition was soon satisfied by unpredictable and lucrative opinions of the sort he had once satirised. By 2010 he could boast: 'I've made more money than I ever thought I would. I've got more readers than I ever thought I would, and more esteem.'[4]

Hitchens had ceased to call himself a socialist by the time he was moved to say, in effect, 'Let's bomb the shit out of them.' In a November 2001 interview with *Reason* magazine he renounced any belief in the existence of 'a general socialist critique of capitalism – certainly not the sort of critique that proposes an alternative or a replacement'. Yet until his full debut as the George W. Bush administration's amanuensis, Hitchens still identified himself in some sense as a man of the left. And even for some interval following his decision to back Bush, Hitchens did not fully renounce his affiliation. Much of the gasp factor in his malediction of the antiwar left derived from his repeated claim that as a lifelong socialist he was calling for cluster bombs in Kabul.

> There has to be a stand made against the worst kind of tyranny that there ever could be, which is religious … You couldn't really have wanted a better and more dynamic and radical confrontation. And the American left decides: 'Let's sit this one out.' That's historical condemnation. To be neutral or indifferent about that, it's just giving up. You just want a quiet life … I still think as an internationalist and as a socialist in what you might call the intellectual, the ethical way – I still do. And I accept also the risks of revolutionary strategy even if it's only a revolution from above.[5]

Predictably unpredictable, then, Hitchens's war against cliché ended in a cliché: he was for bombing them after all. Moreover, Hitchens's stance held a tendency towards the 'moral knight-errantry' that Alasdair MacIntyre had detected in an earlier strain of ex-Communist.[6] Such defectors, often reacting to the austere controlling regimes within the official Communist parties that they had left, sometimes resorted to a moral individualism in which their critique of Stalinism was reduced to a statement of conscience: 'Here I stand. I can do no other.' Rejecting the orthodoxy of high Stalinism, in which morality was deliquesced into iron historical law, the defectors affirmed that the individual was the sole source of virtue. But the illusion of moral independence came at the high cost of reducing their critique to arbitrariness. This made them 'the moral Quixotes of the age'.[7]

Of course, Hitchens had never been a member of a Communist Party, far less the victim of a Stalinist regime. He was, first of all, a left-wing member of the Labour Party until he was expelled because of his activism against the Vietnam War (1965–67). Then for about seven years he was an International Socialist (1967–74), then a member of the Labour Party most likely until his move to the United States (1975–81), and for the majority of his remaining time on the left he was a member of no party or tendency. The sociological basis, as it were, for his leftism was the radical intelligentsia. His main point of contact with these informal circuits in the United States had been Alexander Cockburn, the son of Claud Cockburn, the radical British journalist; as a radical émigré writer in the United States, the younger Cockburn was something of a paragon for the young Hitchens.[8] But once Hitchens was established, he could be said to have had no particular dependency on anyone of the left, and only his employers – the *Nation*, *London Review of Books*, Verso Books, *Vanity Fair* from the early 1990s, and other occasional patrons in the newspaper and television circuit – had any possible hold over him. So when Hitchens spoke of casting aside his chains of political and ideological fealty, these were the chains of leftist conscience rather than organisational or institutional binds.

Nonetheless, it was very important for him to represent his stance as precisely an affirmation of that conscience. And since Hitchens was not joined in his defection by any major faction of the left, either in the United States or elsewhere, this necessarily entailed the suggestion that power had corrupted almost the entirety of the left, which had purchased its plot in the status quo and was anxious to preserve it. In Hitchens's account of his life and writing, he was always one step ahead of the fools.

Other tendencies did manifest themselves. One, which MacIntyre also identified, was to substitute one group affiliation for another – from class struggle to religion, say, or country or 'race'. In Hitchens's case *amor patriae* took the place of socialist confraternity. Likewise, the old habits of a certain kind of vulgar historicism came to Hitchens's aid. This is extremely important in understanding Hitchens's unique political psychology. For one of the things that he often meant by *Marxism* was a sense of history as a narrative of progress. In Hitchens's hands this was rather crude and mechanistic, and tended to express contempt for those on the losing side. As Adam Shatz, a former colleague at the *Nation*, explained:

> Hitchens is drawn to dynamism, to the forces that are actually reshaping the world. I suspect that to him the radical Left increasingly looked like a group of outsiders, losers, and he was tired of the association. It was a short step to embracing revolutionary neoconservatism, which had energy and power on its side.[9]

This must be borne in mind in connection with the slightly *ouvrieriste* strain in Hitchens's politics that persisted in a muted form even after his defection. Even if he did not necessarily have much sympathy for the poor, he respected the organised working class and admired its capacity as an historical force. When he decided that it was no longer such a force, allying with the forces of the right in the American state became a more attractive proposition.

The episodes in Hitchens's trajectory to the right are well known: *l'affaire* Rushdie, the Bosnia wars, the skirmishes with the Clinton White House, and finally the September 11 attacks. The main conclusions that Hitchens drew from these milestones were that religion, specifically Islam, constituted an underestimated force for evil in world affairs, that the US empire could be a countervailing force for good, and that the left comprised herbivores and unprincipled opportunists who had found themselves detached from any international working-class movement capable of challenging capitalism and thus was on the wrong side of history.

This combination of views was not cut entirely from new cloth. Rather, components of his long-standing beliefs took up enlarged roles in a new ideological articulation. His fascination with America, his antitheism (or theophobia, as it might be called, since it plays a role analogous to that of 'Stalinophobia' during the Cold War), his condescending attitude towards the actually existing left, and his faith in empire (for example, his support for Britain during the Falklands War) had long been elements of his worldview. Similarly, his enthrallment with the right, as the truly revolutionary, dynamic force, can be detected in his writings about Thatcherism and indeed Mrs Thatcher herself ('pure sex', he vouched).

Yet for all his inconsistencies Hitchens is a recognisable type: a left-wing defector with a soft spot for empire. He would not be wholly out of place among a century of renegades, including John Spargo, Max Eastman, James Burnham, or Irving Kristol. Indeed, the issues of imperialism and nationalism, so critical to Hitchens's development, were central to the defection of leftists throughout the twentieth century. Leftists often become ex-leftists at the moment they perceive the militarised nation-state as the appropriate defender of progress or democracy. As such Hitchens represents a potentially fascinating instance of a significant political category, well worth examining in his own right, and as an example of something broader.

A MAN OF THE RIGHT

Christopher Hitchens was known as a man of the left. But he was too complex a thinker to be placed on a single left–right dimension. He was a one-off: unclassifiable… You never knew what he would say about anything until you heard him say it.

– Richard Dawkins, 'Illness Made Hitchens a Symbol'

Despite Hitchens's idiosyncrasies, the attempt to represent him as anything other than a conservative in the last ten years of his life rests far too much on his own largely sentimental attachment to the rhetoric of left-wing internationalism and is equally too much informed by his mistaken view of conservatism as simply a force for the status quo. In this book I argue that not only was Hitchens a man of the right in his last years, but his predilections for a certain kind of right-wing radicalism – the most compelling recent example of which was the Bush administration's invasion of Iraq – pre-dated his apostasy.

Certainly, a cliché of conservative thought is that it venerates tradition, which is itself a prima facie cause for suspecting the idea. As Ted Honderich has shown, the notion has the decided disadvantage of representing conservative ideology as mere stupidity – the attachment to the familiar regardless of how absurd or intolerable it is. In fact, conservatism, Corey Robin argues, is distinguished not by an appeal to tradition or the gradual emendation and improvement of the status quo but by violent adventurism, brutal modernism, and the desire to radically transform the status quo the better to preserve it. Conservatism, as an ideology of reaction, reviles the status quo precisely for its inadequacy in the face of revolutionary challenge. From Burke onwards, conservatism has been adept at appropriating the ideas and modes of organisation of the Left, for essentially counterrevolutionary purposes: whether it is Joseph de Maistre's appeal to "*citoyens*" or the neoconservative appropriation of internationalist rhetoric.[10]

This latter tendency can be seen clearly in the case on which Hitchens staked his new creed, the invasion of Iraq. Hitchens justified his support for the venture on multiple grounds, but the keynotes were humanitarian and liberal. The Ba'athist regime was an unusually repressive dictatorship that had perpetrated a genocide against the Kurds. The US was, for all its faults, a pluralist society that would impose the same on Iraq. More broadly, America had found itself 'at war with the forces of reaction' since September 2001.[11] Hitchens suggested that the neoconservatives were the radicals and the antiwar leftists were conservative. He was for 'revolution from above', the peaceniks for the status quo antebellum.

The invocation of the concept of revolution from above is, in this context, telling. Hitchens was, not for the first time, mining the conceptual repertoire of his former Trotskyism to justify his present stance. In the critical idiom of Marxism in which Hitchens was educated, a revolution from above is an historically specific set of political and economic changes imposed on a society by its rulers, or a faction thereof, that establish in a hitherto precapitalist society the bases for an independent centre of capital accumulation. One can think of the Prussian-led construction of the German nation-state as an example of this. Clearly, this would have no bearing on events in Iraq since 2003. Another connotation, as Hitchens would have been well aware, is the establishment by force of 'People's Democracies' in Eastern Europe after World War II. Revolution from above in this sense referred to Stalinist expansionism. But as Hitchens explained in his own plea for 'regime change', his own use of the term referred to 'what colonial idealists used to call the "civilizing mission" '.[12]

As the invasion of Iraq approached, and Hitchens joined the Committee for the Liberation of Iraq, demanding the final extension and conclusion of Operation Desert Storm (a war he had always argued was imperialist) along neoconservative lines, he extolled a 'new imperialism', whose sole remit was to enable local populations to govern themselves. In fact, as the reference to the civilising mission suggests, there was absolutely *nothing* new about justifying imperialism in such terms. Still, 'if the United States will declare out loud for empire, it had better be in its capacity as a Thomas Paine arsenal, or at the very least a Jeffersonian one.'[13]

The moral rearmament of imperialism along these lines was a hallmark, not of radicalism but of neoconservatism. It was the neocons who pioneered the hypocritical 'human rights' discourse that justified Reaganite revanchism in the 1980s, they who coined the conceit of 'democracy promotion' as part of a new, technocratic idiom to justify counterrevolutionary policies in Latin America and elsewhere.[14] If, in doing so, they appropriated some of the vernacular of leftist internationalism, they did so in the tradition of Wilsonian internationalism, itself elaborated as a response to, and attempted containment of, the revolutionary internationalism of the Bolsheviks.[15] This discourse was pioneered by those whose aim was not to revolutionise the world system but to conserve the hierarchies that had been challenged by anticolonial movements. In short, Hitchens's support for the restoration of empire, taking advantage of the senescence of an Arab nationalism that had once been America's major regional foe, was decidedly in the tradition of conservatism.

There was also a thrill at the prospect of mass destruction in Hitchens's rhetoric, another of the things that he meant by 'radical'. He was desperate to prepare America for the sacrifices necessary in the sweeping civilisational combat between the 'West' and its purported enemies which he proposed. 'Frankly,' he said, recalling the spectacle of people leaping from the flaming World Trade Center towers, as they began to swoon, it's

> not that terrifying … That kind of thing happens in a war, it has to be expected in a war, if you're in a war you're gonna lose a building or a plane, and maybe a small town or a school or – you should reckon about once a week. Get ready for it.[16]

I have previously characterised this ideology as a descendant of European *Kriegsideologie*, a martial discourse that emerged on the right in World War I, was sustained by fascism in the interwar period, and had its consummation in World War II. But it has also distinctly American roots – in the racialised social Darwinism and the 'creative destruction' of manifest destiny that permeated both conservatism and the dominant liberalism of the nineteenth and early twentieth centuries. The neoconservative Michael Ledeen was one of the few neocons to openly articulate a vision similar to Hitchens's, that the US would act as a revolutionary bulwark in the Middle East. Ledeen estimated that this legacy of creative destruction was what made America a truly revolutionary society, and he challenged the left's claim to a monopoly on the revolutionary tradition.[17]

It is also worth recalling that even when Hitchens was occasionally revulsed by the right in his later years, it was usually the religious right that he belaboured while defending the modern liberal right. Meanwhile, his loyalty to the United States would no longer permit him 'critical support' for a leftist regime in its crosshairs. Unlike the Sandinistas, for example – or even, at one stage, Saddam Hussein – Hugo Chávez was given no indulgence by Hitchens. 'Getting to know the General', Hitchens said of a photograph depicting his meeting with Chávez and described him as a dictator.[18] For the record, Chávez never held the post of general; his title when Hitchens met him would have been the civilian one of president. The dictator charge was particularly obtuse, given that, when Hitchens met him, Chávez would not have been in office had his supporters not thwarted a US-supported right-wing coup in 2002 that cleared the way for him to run in and win free elections in 2004 and 2008.

Likewise, when Hitchens remonstrated that 'Venezuelan television was compelled to run images of Bolívar, followed by footage of the remains, and then pictures of the boss' to underscore Chávez's claimed political lineage, Hitchens should have known that Venezuelan television is overwhelmingly privately owned, is hostile to Chávez (much of it had participated in the 2002 coup), and is not compelled to run anything by him.[19] Hitchens elsewhere lamented that socialism no longer existed except in the 'forms of populism and nationalism à la Hugo Chávez that seemed to me repellent'.[20] In context, the populist aspect of this couplet is most likely what offended Hitchens, as nationalism was his new creed.

Indeed, apart from Chávez's international alignments and anti-imperialist stance, it seems to have been the Chávez administration's redistribution of wealth that offended Hitchens most and drew invocations of Peronism:

> He would be a tin-pot, crack-pot … just to provide fodder for cartoonists if he didn't a) have a great deal of oil, if he didn't b) make regular visits to Tehran … and if he wasn't trying to replace Fidel Castro, whose bills he's been paying for a very long time. All of this makes him a little bit less of a clown than he looks. Juan Peron and his terrible wife Evita were tremendous nuisances who, like Chávez, paid their voters out of their own Treasury and bribed and corrupted their state into bankruptcy and shame, but they didn't have oil.[21]

Even Aristide was no longer defensible when the US took it upon itself to support a coup d'état in Haiti and coordinate a multilateral intervention that brought death squad leaders and sweatshop owners to power in 2004. Asked to comment on the way in which Clintonite intervention in 1994 seemed to have gone awry, Hitchens remarked: 'I remember in that campaign, actually, the campaign that brought Clinton to power, remember Pat Buchanan ran – leading Catholic right-winger – and his phrase was always for Aristide – "that dingbat priest". A lot of people overestimated Mr Aristide's honesty and capability.'[22] This was a remarkable statement for someone who had earlier used the example of Haiti, and the Clinton administration's conditional ending of the proxy war against the popular movements there, to justify his support for 'humanitarian intervention'.

Little in all this could not have come from the mouth or pen of a Bush administration flack, modifying and rephrasing the anticommunist bromides of the 1980s counterrevolution in Central America. Traces of Hitchens's old leftism resurfaced at moments, particularly following the credit crunch. But by that point Hitchens's nationalism was immovable, and he could not help but see in the miraculous achievements of America's imperialist armies a counterpoint to the decrepitude of its domestic institutions. Any critique implied in this stance is more akin to Irving Kristol's *Two Cheers for Capitalism* than to *Das Kapital*.

Hitchens's claim to have gone beyond the valences of left and right, to have no ideological affiliation, was thus facile. Nor can the claim be rescued simply by referring to Hitchens's refusal to repudiate his past or his tendency to opportunistically strip-mine the cynosures of his old faith in order to defend his new alignments in the conjuncture of the 'war on terror'. It is typical of left–right defectors to claim that they bear witness to a truer realisation of their old values in a more sustainable context. And, in this as in many other respects, Hitchens was predictable as hell.

A BRIEF EXCURSUS ON APOSTASY

Three great waves of left–right defection occurred in the twentieth century. The first was during and after World War I and the Russian Revolution. Its major sites were in western Europe, as the continent's socialists capitulated to an imperialist war that they were sworn to oppose. Not every socialist who joined the nationalist frenzies gravitated to the right, but a minority did. Among the prizefighters of this wave of anticommunist reaction were Gustave Hervé in France, the hysterical antimilitarist who had become a 'national socialist'; Benito Mussolini in Italy, the syndicalist who had turned into a pioneer of fascism; and John Spargo in the United States, the Hyndmanite socialist who proceeded gradually through Bernsteinian revisionism, Christian socialism, and Wilsonian anticommunism, before supporting Franco in the Spanish Civil War, and concluding his life as a supporter of Barry Goldwater.[23]

The second and third were at two pivotal moments of the Cold War, with their locus largely in the United States. These were in the immediate aftermath of World War II, as former Communists, Trotskyists, and left-liberals made their adjustments to the Cold War, and in response to the civil rights and antiwar movements that crested about twenty years later, with the neoconservatives. Some of the same figures – notably, Irving Kristol and Daniel Bell – populated both camps of reaction, first becoming Cold War liberals, then neoconservatives. But while the cold warriors comprised a broad and ascendant political bloc, with ex-communists forming the vanguard, the neoconservatives arose amid the breakdown of the Cold War consensus and the revival of leftist politics.

As a result the ex-communists could be more single-mindedly focused on the international struggle against the Soviet Union, while the politics of neoconservatism were far more substantially inscribed by domestic struggles on issues ranging from race to education – a fact reflected in the ensuing culture wars.

This is to state things in an extremely schematic fashion. In reality turns to the right among the intelligentsia were drawn-out processes punctuated by miniwaves and with distinct temporalities in each society. For example, while the neoconservatives began to take shape in the United States in the wake of the civil rights movement, the French 'antitotalitarians' emerged from their Maoist chrysalis in the mid-1970s as the struggles unleashed after May 1968 subsided. Similarly, in the UK a new generation of reactionaries emerged amid the crisis of social democracy and particularly the 'winter of discontent'. During that nadir 'former leftwingers such as Kingsley Amis, Max Beloff, Reg Prentice, Paul Johnson and Alun Chalfont anthologised their apostasy in a book proudly titled *Right Turn*. Most of these would find themselves comfortably in the Thatcherite camp. Another of their number, Robert Conquest, even spent time as Mrs Thatcher's speechwriter.[24]

Hitchens, a member of the *soixant-huitard* generation, could well have defected along with many of his peers in the late 1970s. Indeed, in this period he was close to that informal sodality of Amis, Conquest, et al., who were defined by their staunch antileftism. And in retrospect it now appears that he did have a certain closeted sympathy for Thatcherism. But resistant to cliché as he then was, he instead moved to the United States and positioned himself as an English radical amid compromising liberals. Even his Falklands fever was somewhat covert and never recorded in an article by him at the time, as far as I can discover. The troupe of David Horowitz and Michael Medved could not tempt him away with the prospect of 'Second Thoughts' in the late 1980s, nor did he immediately join the Fukuyama-ites in proclaiming the 'end of history' when Stalinism toppled over. Aloof from, and seemingly insusceptible to, the gravitational pull of the right, Hitchens nonetheless proceeded to make a gradual rapprochement throughout the 1990s, so that what remained of his leftism could not withstand the challenge by the aerial assault of a handful of motivated jihadis.

The point here is not to identify a tradition of apostasy extending to Washington, DC, circa 2001. It would be absurd to situate Hitchens in any proximity to Mussolini or Hervé, although Hitchens was closer to Spargo and Kristol than he might have been willing to admit. Such defections are historically specific. Even if they draw on the archives of past ideologies – as, for example, the former leftists who signed up for the war on terror and donned the discursive regalia of the Cold War ex-communists – their defection arises from the unfolding of present conditions and their crises. Nevertheless, certain structural similarities in the secessions of each generation deserve attention.

First is the ever-present context of empire and militarism, which, in its different forms, is implicated in each of the waves I have identified. The emphases of different left–right defectors vary, but the issue of international order is an almost constant factor, as is the existence of a Bogey-Scapegoat that can absorb the blame for its chaotic violence. Second, and relatedly, defectors have a propensity to become nationalistic. This is often because in the context of war, or interimperialist rivalry, the nation itself is both threatened and seen as the bulwark against a threat to survival. Socialists often begin their journey to the right when they begin to identify their national state with the prospects for civilisation. Third, as neophyte reactionaries who have suddenly found that they have spent much of their lives working for the wrong side, they prosecute the war against their former confederates far more viciously and devotedly than their newfound allies. Finally, with the turn to the right comes the promulgation of a new theodicy, a manichean doctrine of good vs evil accompanied by a less-than-sanguine appraisal of humanity. From Reinhold Niebuhr's 'Children of Darkness/Children of Light' dichotomy – pioneered for Cold War ideology, which also underpinned neoconservative ideology – to the 'liberalism of fear' developed by Judith Shklar and taken up by the ex-Trotskyist Kanan Makiya, such ideological metaphors occupy a central role in antitotalitarian doctrine. The effect of this is profoundly conservative, since its suspicion of what is called utopian thinking – the sort Hitchens derided as 'sinister perfectionism' – ultimately proves to be hostile to any but the most gradual and cautious social transformation.[25]

On each of these points Hitchens proved an exceedingly typical apostate. In truth, it is not hard to see him in the Isaac Deutscher essay Hitchens referenced in reviewing the Second Thoughts conference:

> He is haunted by a vague sense that he has betrayed either his former ideals or the ideals of bourgeois society; like Koestler, he may even have an ambivalent notion that he has betrayed both. He then tries to suppress his sense of guilt and uncertainty, or to camouflage it by a show of extraordinary certitude and frantic aggressiveness. He insists that the

world should recognise his uneasy conscience as the clearest conscience of them all.

But there is a crucial difference. Deutscher was describing the ex-communists with some sympathy. He understood their sense of betrayal. In their horrified revulsion they were similar to Beethoven and Wordsworth, who resiled on hearing that Napoleon had made himself emperor – an act they regarded as a defeat for humanity. The ex-communists too had seen such a reversal, as the supposedly revolutionary state of Russia forged alliances with Hitler and purged the revolutionaries from Soviet ranks. 'There can be no greater tragedy', Deutscher said,

> than that of a great revolution's succumbing to the mailed fist that was to defend it from its enemies. There can be no spectacle as disgusting as that of a post-revolutionary tyranny dressed up in the banners of liberty. The ex-Communist is morally as justified as was the ex-Jacobin in revealing and revolting against that spectacle.[26]

But Hitchens was coping with no great betrayal, despite his laboured pretence to the contrary. Nor was there anything comparable to the USSR and Warsaw Pact. The histrionics of the Cold War liberals and neocons had been over-the-top about that supposed threat to the 'free world'. So, how was it that Hitchens had sailed through the Cold War without greatly panicking but nonetheless conjured a civilisational challenge out of a handful of combatants with box cutters?

A MAN IN FULL

This is not a biography but an extended political essay. Therefore I am less interested than most reviewers and columnists in raking through Hitchens's familial affairs, sex life, and circles of friendship and influence. Yet one cannot ignore these things completely. For all his distaste for the slogan 'the personal is political', Hitchens applied it and lived it to the full. Whether it was Mother Teresa, Bill Clinton, or George Galloway, Hitchens's foil had to be shown as an out-and-out unprincipled, mediocre, physically repulsive mountebank. In fairness, Hitchens might have struggled if those standards were applied to him, even before he wound up spinning for President Bush, until there was no one left to lie for. But Hitchens was a great sentimentalist, and his approach to politics was profoundly visceral and instinctual.

To evaluate Hitchens's politics is to attempt at least some assessment on the type of person he was. His judgement of character – those he chose as friends as well as allies, and those he chose to make enemies or travesty of – is also inseparable from his political development. It is, then, another measure of the declension of his faculties and of his probity. It is one thing to sell out Sidney Blumenthal to the GOP, but to exchange Edward Said for Ahmed Chalabi? To smear Noam Chomsky yet endear oneself to Paul Wolfowitz?

Who, then, was 'the Hitch'? He was, in an idiom he would have understood, a petty bourgeois individualist who esteemed collectivism at least some of the time but never submitted to it himself. He resented the rich and powerful but enjoyed their company, and he sympathised with the radical working class while lacking pity for the poor. He was rarely deferential, unless it was to the military, but enjoyed abusing social inferiors – his habit of being rude to waiters, perhaps in emulation of the journalist Pappenhacker in Evelyn Waugh's *Scoop*.[27] Hitchens was known as an exceptionally warm and generous person by some of his friends but could also be callous to the point of cruel if crossed. A gregarious conversationalist who sustained intense friendships with a small coterie of litterateurs, someone who summoned and expected loyalty, he could unflinchingly betray those he declared were among his closest friends.

As a writer whose gratuitous self-display was nonetheless always selective, he could tactfully conceal aspects of himself. Yet by several accounts he could be trusted with no secret divulged by anyone. He hated the oppression of women by religion but was indulgent of other varieties of misogyny, particularly that passing itself off as wit. A professional ironist, he descended at times into low contrarianism or into depths of puce-faced literalism. His intellect was greatly overvalued in his later years, and he was prone to bouts of unimpressive philistinism. As someone who despised the sentimentality in certain quarters of the left, he was a purveyor of finely honed sentiment, devastatingly quick on his feet with emotionally potent oversimplification but also given to nauseating platitude. He was a gifted writer but also rather lazy at times, sometimes appearing to borrow material from others and not always with attribution. And as someone with uncommonly wide reading, he often lacked depth, either unable or unwilling to cope with the sorts of complex ideas that he occasionally attempted to criticise.

Last, he was cosmopolitan with a profoundly chauvinistic streak, an ouvrieriste with a closet sympathy for Thatcherism (particularly its libertarian, free-market wing), and a progressive imperialist in the tradition of Mill, Tocqueville, Roosevelt, and Wilson who fancied that the US military was the last genuine repository of republican virtue in a decaying liberal capitalism.

Perhaps my point is obvious. One cannot begin to describe Hitchens's personality without adumbrating his public stances; likewise, none of these stances can be detached from the person he was. Insofar as it attempts to assay the Hitchensian idiolect, this book does attempt to be either exhaustively biographical nor encyclopaedic in their analysis. On the contrary, it lives up to its subtitle. 'The Trial of Christopher Hitchens' is, yes, a pun, intended to evoke how the author became, to a degree, what he had loathed. But it is also a literal brief: this is unabashedly a prosecution. And if it must be conducted with the subject in absentia, as it were, it will not be carried out with less vim as a result.

ADDENDUM, ON THE COMPLETE AND UTTER WORKS

I have alluded to Hitchens's propensity for appropriating the ideas and work of others with either oblique or no acknowledgement. In these pages I am evaluating Hitchens's writing chiefly on its political merits. However, part of the charge I make is that in his journalism, and in his writing more broadly, his standards of evidence and rigour underwent a serious decline as he turned to the right. And this case cannot be made without discussing, at least briefly, the weaknesses in his approach that were already apparent.

It is fair to say that much of Hitchens's writing consisted of self-plagiarism. There was rarely a good line that did not get more than one airing, while *Hitch-22* is made up significantly of anecdotes and arguments published in previous essays. There is no shame in this: he was eminently quotable. The fact is, though, that at least some of what was most laudable in Hitchens's output was probably not his own work.

One reviewer has already detected plagiarism in the case of large tranches of *Thomas Paine's Rights of Man*, a late book and probably a somewhat opuscular component of the Hitchensian oeuvre.[28] The historian Noel Malcolm made a similar allegation about passages in the much earlier *The Parthenon Marbles* that he said were similar to passages in earlier published work by the much more authoritative William St Clair – although Hitchens rebutted the allegation.[29]

I argue that a similar problem exists in the Hitchens volume from which I have drawn my subtitle: *The Trial of Henry Kissinger*. The book was sharp, witty, and devastating for Kissinger, demonstrating to any reasonable person's satisfaction that he was a war criminal, to say the least of it. Glowingly reviewed, and with an accompanying documentary by Eugene Jarecki, this book was critical to expanding Hitchens's audience and for a brief time upholding his reputation as a critic of US power even as he swung behind the Bush administration. These are its known credentials.

Among its lesser-known qualities is the way it used its sources. The acknowledgements pages allude delphically to 'borrowings' from 'more original and more courageous work' by such authors as Lucy Komisar, Mark Hertsgaard, Fred Branfman, Kevin Buckley, and Lawrence Lifschultz. Hitchens also mentioned a general indebtedness to Seymour Hersh, whose work, especially *The Price of Power: Kissinger in the White House*, does seem to have formed the basis for many of the Hitchens book's claims. This is not a standard form of citation, but it can be assumed that Hitchens did not expect those sources to object. Moreover, this simply reflected how Hitchens, who never included such apparatuses as footnotes or bibliographies in his texts, did business. As a journalist he circulated among the relevant cohort, listened to their story over a few drinks, and then wrote up, almost word for word, what he had been told. To this extent his habits are perfectly comprehensible. However, at least some borrowing is given not even this much acknowledgement, such as the lifting from Noam Chomsky and Edward S. Herman's *The Washington Connection and Third World Fascism* in Hitchens's essay 'Kissinger's War Crimes in Indochina'.[30]

A different story obtains with *The Missionary Position* (1995), which experienced a crescendo of fame as a result of the attention paid to *God Is Not Great* (2007). The former was an intelligently written, if slight, polemic, released as an accompaniment to a documentary Hitchens had made on Mother Teresa, proving that she was a friend of poverty, not the poor, and an ally and alibi to dictators, the corrupt, wealthy, and reactionary. But an Indian author produced most of the original research for *The Missionary Position*. The manuscript was judged to need rewriting, and was purchased by Verso with the intention of offering the idea to an Anglophone author. Hitchens, with his acknowledged contempt for religion and propensity for refined iconoclasm, could hardly have been more well suited. What he produced was an intelligently written indictment, but the original hardback made no acknowledgement of the input of several colleagues.[31]

Subtler forms of unacknowledged appropriation, or borrowing without attribution, occur elsewhere in Hitchens's oeuvre. For example, a great deal of his work on Bill Clinton's betrayal on health care was lifted from Sam Husseini's original journalism.[32] A reasonable response to all this might be to stress that Hitchens had himself pinned his colours firmly to the mast by writing 'In Defence of Plagiarism'. 'Where would most of our culture be', he asked, 'without borrowing, adaptation, and derivatives?'[33] Moreover, in most cases of borrowing he was most likely aware that he could rely on the goodwill of his sources towards his project, whether he chose to acknowledge them or not.[34] Nor does any of this deny Hitchens's considerable advantages as a writer and debater – precisely those advantages allowed him to take what others had researched and present it in a perhaps more digestible format.

However, the issue cannot be avoided. First, if Hitchens was used to restating in an accessible form the more courageous and original work of others, if this was in fact how he formed his analyses, what would become of his insight when he had to rely on the cheap foreign policy wisdom of those whom he had once called 'neoconservative ratbags'?[35] Second, such a lax approach in his work cannot be extricated from certain slapdash polemical habits that came to the fore in his later phase. If Hitchens was unaccustomed to normal citation procedures in political writing, and thus did not expect to have his sources queried and checked, the temptation not only to plagiarise but also to, shall we say, overstate certain claims, or overinterpret the claims of others, could be considerable.

This also raises the question of the reliability of his claims. In some of what follows, I demonstrate that Hitchens was untrustworthy, often to the point of travesty, in many of his attributions and imputations. I make this case mainly about his writing after his defection to the right, but I also maintain throughout that none of Hitchens's obvious flaws in the last ten years of his life could simply have emerged *ex nihilo*. Whether or not it was true that Hitchens could be a 'terrific fibber', as his former confrere Alexander Cockburn wrote in 1999, there certainly seem to have been occasions when Hitchens did not scruple to misrepresent an opponent.[36] Again, this was easy enough to do if one had no expectation of being held to account. But his misrepresentation is all the easier to criticise, because Hitchens held to a standard by which it *could* be criticised: both in a performative sense, in that some of his earlier writing is a model of careful, forensic engagement, and in a rhetorical sense, since Hitchens frequently took opponents to task for being careless or dishonest in debate.

Hitchens was in the end a terrible liar, in both senses. He lied egregiously about important matters and about people who deserved better. And he lied carelessly, sloppily, in ways that an attentive reader would notice. Having decided that the American Revolution was the only one left standing, its legacy still vitally relevant, he made the illogical leap of treating the Bush administration as if it were a revolutionary party and he its John Reed. Neither party could live up to such a standard. But Hitchens did not resile from a quantum of revolutionary realpolitik, evidently including the propagation of necessary illusions – less John Reed, more Walter Duranty. In sum, Hitchens was a propagandist for the American empire, a defamer of its opponents, and someone who suffered the injury this did to his probity and prose as so much collateral damage. The late Christopher Hitchens was late before his time.

1 CHRISTOPHER HITCHENS IN THEORY AND PRACTICE

In the advanced capitalist world from the mid-1960s a generation of intellectuals was radicalized and won for Marxism. Many of them were disappointed in the hopes they formed – some of these wild but let that pass – and for a good while now we have been witnessing a procession of erstwhile Marxists, a sizeable portion of the generational current they shared in creating, in the business of finding their way 'out' and away. This exit is always presented, naturally, in the guise of an intellectual advance. Those of us unpersuaded of it cannot but remind its proponents of what they once knew but seem instantly to forget as they make their exit, namely, that the evolution of ideas has a social and material context.

– Norman Geras, 'Post-Marxism?'

Marxism … had its intellectual and philosophical and ethical glories, but they were in the past … There are days when I miss my old convictions as if they were an amputated limb. But in general I feel better, and no less radical, and you will feel better too, I guarantee, once you leave hold of the doctrinaire and allow your chainless mind to do its own thinking.

– Christopher Hitchens, *God Is Not Great*

PERMANENT CONTRADICTION

One vile antithesis, a living and ignominious satire on himself.
– William Hazlitt, *Sketches and Essays*

The amazing, turbulent effect of the French Revolution and the subsequent Napoleonic wars on a certain type of intellectual led William Hazlitt to write 'On Consistency of Opinion'. His comportment was that of a suave and slightly aloof radical raising a disconcerted eyebrow at the 'sudden and violent changes of principle' that these intellectuals had displayed on such trifling matters as the absolute right of the Bourbons to possess France. Wordsworth's passage from Paineite revolutionary politics to Burkean conservatism had been a case in point. Hazlitt observed that those most susceptible to such transformations were in general not those who seemed the most yielding in argument; on the contrary, they were 'exclusive, bigoted and intolerant'. This was because, Hazlitt proposed, those who were least capable of sympathetic investment in the points of view of others were the most likely to be hit with 'double force' when the unexpected happened.

This is plausible: those who are not serious in the positions they occupy are more likely to abdicate them in sudden revulsion when events test their beliefs. We can readily think of political defectors from our own era whose account of the beliefs they once held is so fantastically crude as to make one wonder how they could have been so childish – and when, if ever, they stopped being so. Yet the early Hitchens was not always lacking in interpretive charity, and he does not seem to have wholly lacked sympathy with certain right-wing tropes before his seeming volte-face.

Hazlitt went on to submit that opinions may reasonably alter over time, but there was no need to 'discard … the common dictates of reason'. A person whose opinion has changed

> need not carry about with him, or be haunted in the persons of others with, the phantoms of his altered principles to loathe and execrate them. He need not (as it were) pass an act of attainder on all his thoughts, hopes, wishes, from youth upwards, to offer them at the shrine of matured servility: he need not become one vile antithesis, a living and ignominious satire on himself.

This is instantly applicable to any number of apostate leftists – Max Eastman, James Burnham, David Horowitz, André Glucksmann, and Paul Johnson, to name only a fractional sample.

But what of the late Christopher Hitchens? Did he not swear, even as he was waving adieu and *bon débarras* to his former comrades, that he had not and did not repudiate his past? Was he not notable for attempting to turn the left's language – of internationalism, justice, and even revolution – against it in the war about the war? Yes, and again, yes. But even if he did not reject his past, he most certainly travestied his principles and poured execration on those who kept the faith. His attacks on Noam Chomsky, and particularly Edward Said, had a detectable element of Hitchens's sacrificing his past affiliations 'at the shrine of matured servility'.

Did Hitchens hew to his old ideas like a religion, so that, having lost his faith, he could be said to have found his reason? The author allowed that the socialist politics he once espoused had had elements of religious experience but assured readers that this was all very much in his past.[1] This was yet another fanciful lapse into cliché on Hitchens's part – in this case the old anticommunist saw of *The God That Failed*. Not to deny that socialism has its credenda, but the beliefs that Hitchens held dearest in his postleft phase – opposition to dictatorship, support for Jeffersonian imperialism – were precisely of a sort one can assert only without proof and as articles of faith.[2] What Hitchens found when he lost the socialist faith was but a Nicene Creed of liberalism.

No wonder, then, that the dominant conceit of *Hitch-22*, the author's departing word on his life and his person, is that of keeping, without shame, 'two sets of books' – the tendency that won him the early cognomen 'Hypocritchens'. Indeed, Hitchens delighted in inhabiting seemingly contradictory positions and defending them with distinction. Yet he simultaneously had a manifest urge to prove his consistency. It was not the complete correspondence of his earlier and later analyses that he wished to defend so much as the consistency of his rectitude. Even as he moved to the right, he remained insistently faithful to an idealised version of Orwell and Leon Trotsky, to the icons of the literary left, and to the paladins of twentieth-century resistance, from the Viet Minh to the African National Congress.

This has something to do with a familiar logic of apostasy I discussed in the prologue. Hitchens's long-time friend James Fenton recalled the way this worked:

> He had to change his mind. And in a way that for many people would be humiliating, because he was completely realigning himself. And so, a certain amount of what that was, was at a high decibel level, saying to the rest of us, 'Well, you have changed, you've all changed, the Left has changed', and so on … making it seem less obvious that his position had changed.[3]

That old line in effect says, 'I didn't leave the party; it left me.' Throughout his career the accounts Hitchens gave of himself and his fealties conformed to this standard. Thus, for example, on leaving the

International Socialists, he gave the reason that he disputed the organisation's support for the more disreputable elements of the far left in the Portuguese Revolution and that it had embarked on a Leninist deviation from its Luxemburgist roots. Later, declaring that the era of socialism was concluded, he remarked that there was no progressive left wing worth allying with since it had sold its soul to Clintonism. At each point at which Hitchens felt compelled to move away from his former persuasions, he in some way emphasised his supposed fidelity to them.

This resulted in an accumulating mass of contradictions in Hitchens's persona that were always managed either through solipsism – in effect, 'I prefer my contradiction to yours' – or by appeal to a petrified historical mandate. This makes it easy to quote Hitchens against himself – as his old friend D. D. Guttenplan put it, 'Too easy to offer much sport'.[4] Rather than sport, however, what we will look for is the contradictions amassing in Hitchens's position, from his early revolutionism to his latter-day recusant-yet-observant posture.

THEY FUCK YOU UP: THE POLITICS OF ASPIRATION

'If there is going to be an upper class in this country,' Hitchens's mother said forcefully, 'then Christopher is going to be in it.' By way of self-explanation he recounted this tale several times in his writing. It was his mother, Yvonne, to whom he was closer than anyone in the world, who had decided his path of advancement. Whether because of petty bourgeois ardour, or the desire of a Jewish woman to make her son 'an Englishman', she insisted that he be given an education otherwise preserved for 'about one percent of the population'.[5] A lower-middle-class Liverpudlian who was fond of wit, as well as booze and fags, a woman of liberal humanitarian politics, Yvonne Hitchens was 'the laugh in the face of bores and purse-mouths and skinflints, the insurance against bigots and prudes'. 'The one unforgivable sin', she occasionally remarked with Wildean disdain, 'is to be boring.' She was also grief-stricken at the thought of anyone addressing 'her firstborn son' 'as if he were a taxi driver or pothole-filler'.[6]

Commander Eric Hitchens bored Yvonne and seems to have been relatively forgettable to his children as well – at least for the duration of their childhood. A stoic commander in the British navy, he was a Tory with, his son suggested, nothing to be Tory about. This latter judgment rests on the idea that the Commander was ultimately a rather downtrodden victim of the class system. But it is difficult to credit. A commander in the Royal Navy is a senior officer and was always so.

It is true that Hitchens describes his father as having progressed from the poorer areas of Portsmouth to the middle class via the navy. It is also true that the son tells a heartstring-plucking story of his father's being involuntarily retired after Suez, just before the pay and pensions of new officers were increased. Yet this injustice would surely still leave Commander Hitchens with a great deal to be Tory about, and it would leave young Christopher able to attend public school and begin his ascension.[7]

Nonetheless, if Hitchens's upbringing was not an impoverished one, it was insecure:

> My mother in particular [urged] that the Hitchenses never sink one inch back down the social incline that we had so arduously ascended. That way led to public or 'council' housing, to the 'rough boys' who would hang around outside cinemas and railway stations, to people who went on strike and thus 'held the country to ransom', and to people who dropped the 'H' at the beginnings of words and used the word 'toilet' when they meant to refer to the 'lavatory'.

This seems to have been behind Hitchens's urge to prove himself socially, the original source of a long-standing chip on his shoulder about the establishment and his exclusion from it.[8]

If the Commander was a Tory, he was still 'a very good man and a worthy and honest and hard-working one'. He was also a powerful and recurring presence in Hitchens's life. Hitchens never pursued a military life. And he was disappointed to discover that he was not cut out to be a soldier, partly because his physical courage had limits. As a result the matter of his fortitude – mental and physical – returned as a habitual concern, as did a certain Blimpishness and instinctive reaction that he imbibed from his father. Eric 'helped me understand the Tory mentality, all the better to combat it and repudiate it', Christopher insisted. But the repudiation was only partial. When the Falklands were invaded by the Argentinian dictatorship, the younger Hitchens found himself outraged at the offence to British power, only to be disappointed by his father's lack of bloodlust. Like many who wished they had fought a war, Christopher Hitchens expended his military passion through verbal bravado; his wife, Carol Blue, summarised the posture: 'I will take some of these people out before I die.' But this background was also responsible for some of Hitchens's insights. When he so sensitively diagnosed the 'John Bullshit' that he found in Larkin's poems and detected at the base of Thatcherism, the diagnosis was based on acute, instinctive recognition.[9]

So there is, in Hitchens's formation, the beginnings of that elemental contradiction he called keeping two sets of books and the beginnings of that urge towards social climbing, the constant search for the right entrée, that led him all the way to the Jefferson Memorial, where he was naturalised as an American citizen by no lesser an American than Michael Chertoff, then secretary of the US Department of Homeland Security.

LIVING TO SOME PURPOSE: HITCHENS AND THE REVOLUTION

Hitchens began his life as a socialist while at a private school in Cambridge. A supporter of the Campaign for Nuclear Disarmament and of the Labour Party, he was precociously articulate. He read avidly and widely but seems to have had a preference early on for literary fiction over, for example, the social sciences, for which it seems probable he had no aptitude. He arrived at university in 1966 near the beginnings of a dramatic expansion of tertiary education in Britain. The number of college students doubled, from 100,000 to 200,000, between 1960 and 1967. Today the student population of the UK is more than two million. The inevitable result was the inclusion of some working-class youth in the expanded system, and that led to a phenomenon evident in each of the advanced capitalist societies in which the trend was registered: an intellectual radicalisation and an increasing challenge to the university authorities, symbolised in the revolt at the Sorbonne in 1968.

Oxford was not quite Paris – more Bourbon than Sorbonne – but its radical students did partake of a sustained challenge to the university authorities, the proctors, whose control of student life and maintenance of a rigid hierarchy between teacher and student was such that students today would not recognise it. Hitchens, having been a supporter of the Labour left, was recruited to the International Socialists by a psycho-analyst named Peter Sedgwick, with whom Hitchens became close.

Hitchens always recalled this period with authentic warmth. And he seems to have been highly regarded as both personable and a tremendous debater. Alex Callinicos recalls that he had an 'easy, accessible manner … but there was a slightly ironical quality about him. One assumed that he was a rascal.'[10]

Yet it would be a great mistake to treat his recollections of this period as gospel. Even if he was often candid about his feelings, Hitchens was certainly capable of redaction and revision. His representation of the IS 'groupuscule' and its politics tended to shade the past with his present opinions. Thus, for example, it is not quite true that he was ever on the brink of becoming a 'full-time organiser'. Former comrades recall that he was involved in the party's bodies, and it was true that younger members were being drafted into all sorts of organising positions in order to cope with the surfeit of strikes, social struggles and protests that characterised the period. But organising was not where his talents lay. If anything, he was notable for his louche indolence and a lack of integration with his student comrades. Likewise, his characterisation of the group as post-Trotskyist and Luxemburgist is not completely without foundation, but it does tend to overstate the case with the prefix *post* and omits to say anything of Leninism, which was an increasingly important aspect of the group's perspective as it grew and adapted to its tentative implantation in the industrial working class.[11]

Hitchens developed a particular fondness for the group's founder, Tony Cliff – the nom de guerre of Ygael Gluckstein, a Palestinian Jewish polymath with a most captivating and excitable manner of speaking. This is recalled by those who knew him. Indeed, Hitchens himself chronicled this in a review article for the *London Review of Books* in 1994, expressing a tender contempt for the state of his old comrades and reminiscing about better days. But by the time Hitchens mined this article for *Hitch-22*, Cliff's appearance was merely perfunctory.[12] This may or may not be related to another aspect of IS ideology that undoubtedly influenced Hitchens – its uncompromising anti-Zionism. Cliff had argued for this position within the British left well before the 1967 war had opened the first fissure over the issue and the 1982 invasion of Lebanon made anti-Zionists out of an appreciable minority of leftists. And while Hitchens continued to be critical at times of Zionism even after his change of allegiances, he tended to omit the issue in his recollections of the IS.[13]

His talent as an orator was spotted while he was studying for his degree at Balliol College, Oxford. He rapidly became, next to Michael Rosen, the 'second most famous person' in the university. Hitchens's friendship with Rosen, in fact, was one of the subjects of his revisionism. In the first edition of *Hitch-22*, he described Rosen as a 'Jewish Communist' and later an 'ex-Stalinist' whose family was 'fatally compromised' by Stalinism. Hitchens added that Rosen had, in a production of Günter Grass's play *The Plebeians Rehearse the Uprising*, 'been more or less compelled to go along with the play-within-the-play that satirized the ghastly East German regime and celebrated the workers' revolt against it that had taken place in 1953'. In fact, Rosen had never been a member of any Communist Party. His parents had been but had walked out in 1957. Rosen's politics were Labour left, and insofar as he gravitated to any other socialist formation, it was the groupuscule with which Hitchens was himself aligned.[14] (Some of this was rewritten for the second edition, but Hitchens left in the claim that Rosen was an ex-Stalinist.)[15]

What accounts for such a petty, mean-spirited slander? Rosen believes it has to do with the way in which Hitchens wished to represent his own trajectory. Many from the generation of *soixant-huitards* that Hitchens knew and admired have died and thus can be idealised safely, constituting no threat to his current posture. But Rosen had known Hitchens and had publicly criticised him for supporting Bush's wars. The smear served Hitchens by demonstrating that this criticism was merely the reflex of an old Stalinist and that he, Hitchens, had always been one step ahead of the fools.

In general, however, Hitchens tended to err on the side of heroically romanticising his past and the figures that peopled it. He recalled Peter Sedgwick, who recruited him to the post-Trotskyist IS, with genuine affection. The same is true of Hitchens's reminiscences of C. L. R. James. Yet the individuals Hitchens described in his memoir, *Hitch-22*, were not exactly political animals but omnitalented gurus whose like has not been seen since. This slightly maudlin portrayal is the obverse of the later demonology, which found the left, and especially the far left, in league with 'Islamic fascism'.

On other matters it may be that he was not distorting. Keeping two sets of books meant closeting his real feelings about certain matters, so that while Hitchens later recalled experiencing a certain displaced patriotism for the United States, even at the height of his sixties *gauchisme*, and real joy that the Stars and Stripes had been planted on the moon, it is most likely that he did not share this with any of his comrades.[16] The nickname that Hitchens's friends and comrades at Oxford gave him acknowledges this aspect of his personality. And certainly, for Hitchens, the double life that it alludes to, the keeping of two sets of books, is seen as a virtue, a creative, dialectical spark.

At some length it seems that Hitchens grew weary of the revolutionary left. The circumstances of his departure from the International Socialists are not wholly clear. Hitchens, explaining his decision to leave, cited the IS's support for a 'dictatorship of the proletariat' during the Portuguese Revolution of 1974–75 and later added that he was uncomfortable with the Leninist direction of the party. In fact, though it is known that he was sympathetic to the position of the internal faction opposed to the growing emphasis on a democratic centralism, he never joined it. Most likely he did not think it worth the effort. He had never been especially doctrinal, was disinclined to get involved in heated internal disputes, and had brighter prospects before him. A former comrade of his, Chris Harman, recalled:

> I don't think there was any point at which Chris Hitchens broke publicly with the IS. My impression was that he went flat out to know the right people to make a career in journalism and began to find us a hindrance.[17]

Another, Alex Callinicos, recounts that Hitchens was increasingly distant from politics. In 1973, he met Hitchens during a row at Oxford over the university giving Pakistani President Zulfikar Ali Bhutto an honorary degree. This was at the end of the bloody Bangladesh war, which the Pakistani army had prosecuted mercilessly. The dons and the students had censured the university over it. And Hitchens 'appeared, looking slightly shady, as he was a friend of Benazir Bhutto … I spoke to him afterward, and he said "do you ever think the sun may suddenly burst and everything we do may be meaningless?" I replied that the reflection seemed to me entirely pointless. But it implied a degree of existential detachment.'[18]

Aside from weariness, Hitchens did have a substantive grievance with the direction of the International Socialists in their decision to support the far left in Portugal's 'Carnation Revolution'. The revolution, beginning with the fall of the dictatorship of Marcello Caetano, was one of the most spectacular moments in European history.[19] Notable for the flourishing of grassroots democracy predicated on workplace occupations, popular newspapers, and mass demonstrations, it was also notable for the role of the armed forces in its leadership. Initially, these were generals and junior officers disaffected by the failure of Portugal's colonial policy, who desired to move towards a modern capitalist democracy with a mixed economy. But as the revolt radicalised, a movement of rank-and-file soldiers developed, with some basis in far-left parties such as the Revolutionary Party of the Proletariat/Revolutionary Brigades (PRP). There were serious reservations in the international left about some of this. The PRP had an elitist, Guevarist streak, tending to rely on military action by an armed minority to bring about social transformation. While some feared that military adventurism would give the right an excuse to inflict a new Chile, the main worry was that it could be the germ of a new Stalinist dictatorship in itself.

Nonetheless, at a critical point, the IS set aside any such reservations and supported the PRP and the rank-and-file soldiers. The basis of this was that a strike wave and a series of mass demonstrations had created a crisis in the military, cleaving it between the officer corps who had overthrown the old dictatorship and the rank-and-file soldiery. The government, led by the Socialist Party, was desperate to contain the growing turbulence and particularly to assert its control of the state machinery. The IS urged the PRP to focus less on armed manoeuvres and more on encouraging the development of popular councils of workers and soldiers, which could be the basis for a new socialist democracy. In the end, the PRP participated in an abortive coup d'état, which gave the right wing the chance to go on the offensive and restore discipline in the military. Hitchens lamented the IS stance, and specifically criticised Callinicos for talking about the 'dictatorship of the proletariat' in this context.[20] Recollecting this period, Hitchens excoriated the party in characteristically bilious terms. It had

> openly allied itself with semi-Baader Meinhof elements in that most open and hopeful of all revolutions: a revolution which can now be seen as the last spasm of 1968 enthusiasm. Not being very choosy politically, the aforesaid elements went in with a stupid and nasty attempted coup, mounted by the associates of the Portuguese Stalinists ... Thus not only had the comrades moved from Luxemburg to the worst of Lenin, but in making this shift of principle they had also changed ships on a falling tide. Time to go. Still, I recollect the empty feeling I had when I quietly cancelled my membership and did a fade. I remember trying to tell myself that I was leaving for the same reasons I had joined. But the relief – at ceasing to hear about 'rank and file' and 'building links' – soon supplanted the guilt.[21]

At any rate, the picture Hitchens gave of fading into the background is accurate. Nor is there any sign that he fell out with his former comrades. Even when he publicly repudiated his old comrades for having inadvertently published an 'anti-Zionist' letter in the party newspaper, *Socialist Worker*, which was in fact written by a member of the National Front, Hitchens retained his sympathy for the organisation. In a letter to John Rose, who then worked on the organ, Hitchens expressed his respect for Tony Cliff.[22] Hitchens continued to speak at the party's meetings when it was known as the Socialist Workers' Party.

Yet, Hitchens was evidently exhausted by both the revolutionary and reformist left in Britain. Having left the IS, he had briefly joined the Labour Party.[23] But he came to resent the 'tax-funded statism' of the old consensus as much as the union bureaucracy and the Labour right. Hitchens later confessed to being physically unable to vote for Labour in 1979 and to having realised that this was because he wanted Thatcher to win. He admired her determination to take on the stale postwar arrangements and was relieved that she could at last do so.[24]

At any rate, he was on the brink of abandoning the small, wet, defeated islands of the United Kingdom and making off for the United States – a surrogate *patria*, so far as Hitchens was concerned, and a more promising prospect for a talented writer.

A COMPOUND IDENTITY: AMERICAN AND JEWISH QUESTIONS

Hitchens had been, before he joined the International Socialists, what he called a 'Left Social Democrat (or "LSD" in the jargon of the movement)'.[25] This, roughly speaking, is the position to which he reverted after leaving amid the backwash of the revolutionary upsurge of 1968. But the state of social democracy was dire, its left was weaker than ever, and Hitchens had a troubling feeling that Thatcher might have a point. Yet if he did not have much faith in the British left, he was increasingly interested in two other, larger political canvases: Third World revolutionary movements, and the United States, to which he emigrated. Hitchens's brief fondness for Saddam – 'the first visionary Arab statesman since Nasser' – was of a piece with the former but so was his far more enduring interest in the issue of Cyprus.[26]

In his early years in America, Hitchens seemed to have moved slightly to the left, barring the brief expostulation of patriotic bullishness over the Falklands/Malvinas. Partly, this may reflect the milieu upon which he was initially dependent – friends such as Alexander Cockburn provided Hitchens's entrées to the New York scene, while his colleagues at the *Nation* were unlikely to be susceptible to any pleading for Mrs Thatcher. But his focus on international struggles also gave him a strong position from which to assail the Reaganites, even if he had no enthusiasm for the Democrats.

D. D. Guttenplan, a correspondent at the *Nation* who knew Hitchens well through the 1980s, recalls that when Hitchens migrated to the United States and began working at the *Nation*, he 'came across as a left internationalist, someone for whom liberation movements were much more important than the internal politics of any country, certainly the US, where he was deeply uninterested in American politics'.

Mike Davis had a similar recollection of Hitchens in the 1990s, as 'a charming and bighearted guy' who 'had a tendency to develop profound emotional attachments to third world groups, particularly the Cypriots and the Kurds, and I think that eventually blinded him to the reality of American wars.'[27]

Yet, if Hitchens's interest in domestic politics was limited, his early writing on US foreign policy did not substantially deviate from an anti-imperialist position. Indeed, he consistently drew a direct relationship between the US invasion of Vietnam and the proxy wars in Central America. But ascending the steep career slope in US media circles also encouraged Hitchens's propensity for ingratiating himself with the chattering class. Guttenplan recalls:

> I remember in '88, I was writing a media column for *New York Newsday*, and there was a fake award which Christopher organised for journalists in Washington called the Osric Award, for the most suck-up journalists. It was a roll-call of shame. They had an awards dinner, and I was invited to report on it … And it was a kind of Washington snark-fest. Most of the people there were vaguely liberal, left-of-centre, but it was much more about attitude than politics. And Christopher was really in his element. You could tell that all these people looked up to him, and thought he was just a swell fellow. I remember thinking, 'This is very clever self-promotion.' If you get publicity for being the person who denounces other people, then you get a kind of power.[28]

In the summer of 1988 Hitchens brought the tidings to his reading public that he was Jewish, or at least of Jewish descent.

'I was pleased', he said, 'to find that I was pleased.' Perhaps Lesley Hazleton erred on an uncharitable interpretation of this by suggesting that he obviously expected another response. But let us recall what he had said about his mother. She was the daughter of Dorothy Levin, who in turn was the daughter of Lionel Levin, who had married the daughter of a Mr Nathaniel Blumenthal, a nineteenth–century Jewish refugee from Poland who had 'married out' but nonetheless raised all his children in the Orthodox manner. This was the basis for Hitchens's claim to Jewish descent. But according to Hitchens, his mother had attempted 'to "pass" as English' in order to avoid being the subject of anti-Semitism. The invocation of the concept of racial passing in this context is odd. By implication his mother was *not* English, because she was Jewish; thus to be English was to be white and Christian. Ironically, Hitchens, in describing his mother's dilemma, performed the racialising gesture that had victimised his grandparents and forced his mother to disavow her lineage.[29]

Moreover, Hitchens had a tendency, particularly in his later writing, to speak of the 'Jewish people' as if they were all implicated in the state of Israel. For example, in the context of a fairly standard argument against Zionism, he added: 'A sixty-year rather botched experiment in marginal quasi-statehood is something that the Jewish people could consider abandoning.'[30] Of course, this is not anti-Semitism in its most toxic sense. But it does remind one that philo-Semitism is a not-too-distant cousin of anti-Semitism (particularly in England). And, when read in conjunction with his critique of Said (see Chapter 2), it does suggest that the latter had a point when he said that Orientalism and anti-Semitism are joined at the hip.[31] Further, an unavoidable aspect of this discovery must be Hitchens's sense of how it would affect his career.

'When I read that piece in *Grand Street*', Guttenplan recalled,

> I remember calling Christopher up and saying, 'Welcome to the club.' But I also remember thinking, when it came out, two things. One was 'Oh, that's useful because Christopher has always been very pro-Palestinian, and much more forthrightly pro-Palestinian than any other non-Palestinian in the US.' And he had edited that collection with Edward Said. And I thought, 'This will make it harder to accuse him of being an anti-Semite.'
>
> I must say I never thought of him as being an anti-Semite, he always struck me as being very scrupulous in his politics. On the other hand, I knew he was friends with a lot of the *New Republic* people. And I thought, 'Well, this is convenient, because it will help him with the *New Republic* people, because a certain amount of eccentricity is tolerated among Jews. That will help him with people like Michael Kinsley and Leon Wieseltier.' And I think to a certain extent that happened. I don't think it happened just because he discovered he was Jewish, but he was taken up by the *New Republic* for a time. Christopher wrote for the *New Republic* and went to their parties.[32]

In a sense, then, the Brit abroad had just acquired a new dimension to his identity, one that may have slightly taken the edge off his anti-Zionism. And it may have made his provocations over the Holocaust slightly less toxic for his audience. One of Hitchens's brief passions in the late 1990s was the defence of the pro-Nazi historian David Irving and, increasingly, Hitchens's sympathy with Irving's view that the numbers of those murdered in the Holocaust have been grossly inflated. Hitchens told anyone who would listen that it would be wrong to dismiss Irving's work, for there was a real issue at stake. To Tariq Ali and quite a few others, Hitchens divulged an interest in making a film about the subject.

> He came to me and said, 'Tariq, do you think six million Jews were killed in the Judeocide?' I said to him, 'What difference does it make?' And he said, 'You're wrong to poo-poo this – the figures don't add up. If it was 4.3 million Jews who were killed, we should use that figure.'[33]

It was not only the figures that Hitchens found dubious but, following Irving, the details of what the Nazis are alleged to have done. Dennis Perrin says Hitchens dismissed 'the concept of lamp shades [made of human skin] and human soap in the Nazi camps as Stalinist propaganda.'[34]

All three issues have a margin of legitimate historical controversy. At the very least, there is disagreement about precisely how many Jews the Nazis murdered and certainly doubt about the extent of human soap-making. But what is suggestive is that Hitchens seems to have believed that he could not engage with the questions from within mainstream historical scholarship and thus needed to hear them from a scholar with a weak spot for Hitlerism. This was, to be fair to Hitchens, before the conclusion of the trial in which Irving was taken to pieces over his fabrications – a libel case he had brought against the historian Deborah Lipstadt because of her characterisation of him as a 'Holocaust denier'. It was also therefore before the publication of the historian Richard J. Evans's *Telling Lies for Hitler*, a crushing demolition of Irving's propaganda.[35]

But even this concession to 'fairness' is an insult to Hitchens, since it implies that he was taken in by Irving. Hitchens had justly criticised H. L. Mencken for his sanguinity in the face of fascism – a 'literary failure' and not just political decrepitude. In the figure of Hitler was a target, a quack, a charlatan, 'a crank to end all quacks', Hitchens declared. 'Such a target! And from the pen that had flayed and punctured the "booboisie", there came little or nothing.'[36] It would be nonsensical to compare to Hitler a petty, duplicitous fraud like Irving, to say nothing of comparing Hitchens to Mencken. But at least we can say that Hitchens knew what a flunk it was to be remiss on the issue of fascist quackery. To make himself an ally of Irving just when the latter's worth as an historian was being mercilessly divested surely immolated Hitchens's probity at the shrine of opportunism. As was often the case with Hitchens, however, rather than recant or express contrition, he rationalised and revised, such that he painted himself mainly as a defender of free speech rather than someone hoping to stir controversy about the Holocaust.[37]

But what to make of this episode, given Hitchens's own statement that 'a Holocaust denier is a Holocaust affirmer'?[38] It might be true, if finger-wagging, to suggest that the author of the 'Homage to Telegraphist Jacobs' was trivial about his recently acquired Jewishness, that it meant as much to him as it can mean to someone who is capable of making a week's reputation out of the paradoxical assertion that a Holocaust affirmer is actually on to something. More prosaically, it suggests that Hitchens was capable of rationalising any absurdity without its affecting his amour propre, provided there were indeed the requisite reputation miles to be earned in the process.

There would be far worse, far more wholesale quackery on Hitchens's part, in the years to come. As I mentioned, quite often in those years he would find himself standing up for the 'Jewish people', whether their foe was real or imaginary. On these occasions Hitchens would freely dispense the trivialising innuendo, implying anti-Semitism on the part of his opponents, an accusation to which he had himself once been subject, and from which the discovery of his Jewishness only partially screened him. Hitchens's Jewish descent thus formed first a protective carapace, then a weapon, but it also arguably formed part of a compound Anglo-American-Jewish identity that distinguished him among his peers.

HATING CLINTON, LOVING BUSH

Hitchens could be unforgiving of slights. When his friend Guttenplan tried to get Hitchens to work at *Vanity Fair*, he was rebuffed by the editor. Guttenplan dealt with this by treating Hitchens to an expensive lunch on the expense account each time he was in town. Hitchens, before eating, routinely checked: 'This *is* on Fuckface, right?'[39] Similarly, his long-standing hatred for the Clintons may have owed at least in part to a rebuff by Hillary Clinton. Soon after Bill Clinton was elected president in 1992, Hitchens approached his friend Tariq Ali with some news. 'I need to discuss something with you,' Hitchens said.

> I've got Jessica Mitford and her husband coming round to dinner in a few weeks' time. You know that Hillary Clinton worked in his law practice as an intern and then as a young lawyer? Well, I've invited Hillary

along to my dinner, and this will be a big test for her, whether she comes or not.

How might it have been had the Clintons decided to entertain Hitchens and taken him into their confidence? Ali's answer: 'He would have been completely playing ball with them.'[40]

If that had happened, Hitchens would not have been the only one to be charmed by the Clintons. 'Clinton did have this capacity to seduce journalists who had until then seemed like outsiders and happy with it,' Guttenplan recalled.

> There was a way in which Clinton seemed, I think mistakenly, to be 'one of us' … I remember people thinking that because this guy worked for McGovern, he demonstrated against the war, so when he gets to be president, he'll be great. I remember thinking, 'This guy comes from Arkansas and he's not a racist, that's such a big thing and it's worth voting for.'[41]

However, it is not obvious that Hitchens was ready to be seduced even before Hillary's rebuff. As soon as the governor of Arkansas appeared as a serious presidential candidate, Hitchens set out to prove to liberals that Clinton was not their man and did so at first primarily by demonstrating that Clinton was, if not a racist himself, quite happy to play to Southern racist traditions.

Exhibit A in this charge was the execution of Rickey Ray Rector. Here was a man against whom punishment was futile, and not merely cruel, as he had already destroyed his frontal lobe with a self-administered gunshot. Hitchens went about showing that not only was death by lethal injection an uncivilised horror, and not only racist in its application, but even by the usual standards of America's barbaric criminal justice system a gross affront to normal standards of clemency. As such the person who authorised this execution – William Jefferson Clinton – could be shown to have 'opted to maintain the foulest traditions and for the meanest purposes', even where no poll-driven exigency was involved.

As to the idea that Clinton was 'one of us', having demonstrated against the Vietnam War, Hitchens pointed out early on that this was something of an embarrassment to Clinton, and he was outflanking the senior Bush to the right on foreign policy.[42]

Once Clinton was elected, he provided material in abundance for Hitchens to continue his assault. The burden of much of what Hitchens would write during the next eight years was straightforwardly leftist. He assailed the Clintons for selling out their voters on health care, showing that they had systematically aligned themselves with the largest health maintenance organisations, devising a policy to suit them while feigning operatic chagrin at the opposition mounted by the smaller and medium-sized health-care companies. (Again, a great deal of this was taken from Sam Husseini, initially without credit.) Hitchens charged Clinton with colluding with the most reactionary forces in American politics to destroy the welfare system and encourage racist scapegoating as the despair piled up. [43] All this was very much the bread and meat of the radical left to which Hitchens remained affiliated.

Yet Hitchens's assault on Clinton, aside from an unexceptionable and unexceptional critique of Clintonite 'triangulation', workfare, and war crimes, was highly personalised. Clinton's character, before his policies, was the subject of Hitchens's prosecution. An element of this had been present from the very beginning of the contretemps. Indeed, Hitchens had always had a tendency to revile the personnel of American statecraft without a great deal of emphasis on the structures of power. Moreover, he coupled this with a tendency to seek feuds, individuals with whom to spark off controversy, the better to remain noticed and noticeable. It is true that there was a rape allegation against Clinton, which Hitchens found credible. But he did not even like Clinton's having consensual sex, as this made him the 'boss who uses subordinates as masturbatory dolls'.[44]

This reached an extraordinary zenith, or nadir, when Hitchens went after Clinton by selling out his friend Sidney Blumenthal. The affair arose over something Blumenthal is alleged to have said during a dinner with Hitchens and his wife, Carol Blue. Blumenthal is supposed to have described Monica Lewinsky, whose affair with Clinton had become the basis of an impeachment of the president, as a stalker. This was at a time when Blumenthal was denying before Congress that he or anyone else in the White House had issued such rumours. Hitchens swore an affidavit that could have put his friend and cousin inside for perjury.

'If I hadn't had some relish for the ironic contrast between the sublime and the ridiculous, I would never have become a friend of Sidney Blumenthal's in the first place', Hitchens vouched in 2003, adding, 'and would never have been pushed to the length that this friendship eventually required of me: a decision to testify that a President who was certifiably filthy in small things might deserve to be arraigned on larger matters also'.[45] As I have shown, one thing that Hitchens tended to mean by *ironic* (or *dialectical*, for that matter) was an ability to have things both ways. His modus operandi had been complaisance towards the rich and influential while reserving the right to lacerate them in print or at his leisure.

But Hitchens had gushed about his comradeship with Blumenthal not long before deciding to swear an affidavit effectively telling Congress that Blumenthal had perjured himself in the House's impeachment proceedings. Despite their disagreements about Clinton, they had 'soldiered against the neoconservative ratbags', Hitchens wrote. 'Our life *à deux* has been, and remains an open book. Do your worst. Nothing will prevent me from gnawing a future bone at his table or, I trust, him from gnawing in return.' As Alexander Cockburn pointed out, 'Hitchens was just writing these loyal lines immediately before the lunch ... whose conversational menu Hitchens would be sharing with these same neoconservative, right-wing ratbags ten months later'.[46]

This would not be the last time that Hitchens would sacrifice a friendship on his journey to the right nor the last time that the result would be a considerable warming of relations with the ratbags, not to mention a further escalation up the career slope. By the late 1990s, amid the Blumenthal scandal, the *Washington Post* noted that the 'Hitchens-Blumenthal brouhaha' was

> a very big story among a very small group of people ... who inhabit a rarefied world where the top pols and bureaucrats sup with the media and literary elite at exclusive dinner parties. It's a cozy little club of confidential sources and off-the-record confidences, and both Hitchens and Blumenthal are members.[47]

Hitchens had drawn closer to the right in the context of fighting the Clinton wars, though he did not generally acknowledge this. This state of affairs was amusingly dramatised in a fan documentary about Hitchens, *Hitch Hike*, that was broadcast in the UK by Channel 4 in 2000. In it comical Tea Party prototypes feted the writer by gushing over Hitchens's criticisms of Clinton, and Hitchens lingered and basked in the solidarity. Grinning much like Webster the cat, pumping hands, and exchanging words, Hitchens left them with the rousing sentiment: 'A republic, if you can keep it!'[48]

But his transfiguration after September 2001 required a much more open embrace of the reactionaries and thus by implication a complete revision, or at least downgrading, of the standards and values against which he had found Clinton so repugnant. The corollary of his defection was that he went from defacing the Clinton presidency to championing one of the most reactionary executives in US history.

'I debated him in Georgetown University on the subject of 9/11', Tariq Ali recalls,

> and it was a different Christopher. Not yet totally transformed, but incredibly hostile, and basically it was an awful debate … Then he chaired a debate on 9/11, in which he intervened nonstop, at the *Los Angeles Times* book fair in Los Angeles. And what I recall on that occasion is, after the authors had spoken, they then went into little cubicles to sign books, and Christopher was in a cubicle next to mine. And he thought I couldn't hear him. And, I'll never forget this, I heard one of his fans asking him, 'Mr Hitchens, do you think that at long last we have a contrarian in the White House?' And Hitchens replied, 'I think you may be right there' – in a soft voice because he didn't want me to hear it. I took him aside after the signing and said, 'This is utterly appalling.' He just walked away.[49]

On almost any issue on which Hitchens could have indicted Clinton – war crimes, poverty, and racism – Bush was in every sense worse than Clinton. Had Clinton overseen the response to Hurricane Katrina as Bush did, for example, Hitchens would not have thought to spare the president his criticism. Had the Bush tax cuts been the Clinton tax cuts, Hitchens would have been on the front line, urging the liberals to pay attention to the larceny. There was no conversation to be had about a Bush health-care betrayal, because the Republican Party would never feign support for socialised medicine. And, as for the death penalty, Hitchens well knew that this was not a strong point for Bush. As Hitchens wrote before the 2000 election, 'The staggering pace of executions in Texas means that Bush has either a) been doing little else but reviewing death sentences or b) been signing death warrants as fast as they can be put in front of him.'[50]

But the far larger task of combatting al-Qaeda, Saddam, and other 'riff-raff' meant that Hitchens no longer had any use for baiting the president. It is true that, initially, he was vaguely disrespectful and even satirical about Bush, zeroing in on the telltale closeness of his eyes and his mangled speech.[51] But this came sharply to a close after 9/11. Instead, Hitchens came to respect the president's dynamism and to resent the bovine ignoramuses calling him a cowboy. Bush had waited a full *five weeks* after the Twin Towers fell before bombing anyone – a more cowboyish president would surely want to 'blow up at least an aspirin factory in Sudan'.[52]

More generally, Hitchens felt that the calamity had brought out the best in Bush. 'The events of Sept. 11, 2001', Hitchens suggested, 'explain the transformation of George Bush from a rather lazy small-government conservative into an interventionist, in almost every sense, politician.'[53] Hitchens's reappraisal of Bush was coterminous with the writer's being serenaded by the administration. Hitchens wound up a courtier, enjoying the patronage of Paul Wolfowitz and reciting the public relations lines developed in the Oval Office and Pentagon.

Hitchens's ego ideal had once been the hero of Nadine Godimer's *Guest of Honour*, who 'sees his beloved revolution besmirched and yet does not feel tempted – entitled might be the better word – to ditch his principles'.[54] His bêtes noires had been those former liberals and socialists who became die-hard counterrevolutionaries: Norman Podhoretz, Conor Cruise O'Brien, and Paul Johnson each were treated to Hitchens's wry scorn. O'Brien's panning was the more lavish because of the generous helpings of more-in-sorrow-than-in-anger head shaking that accompanied it. The worst of it, perhaps, was that reaction was almost invariably accompanied by a declension in the prose. O'Brien could 'descry, in the features of a ruling elite, the lineaments of an oppressed minority' but only by means of tortuous analogies, contradictory postures, and absurdities.[55]

By 2002 Hitchens had found himself in the ranks of a beleaguered minority of radicals who wanted to revolutionise Iraq – a minority that included only the Republican Party, the Pentagon, most of Congress, the majority of the US media, and the British and Israeli governments – against a 'respectable status quo' on the left.[56]

CODA: THE 'MATERIALIST THEORY OF HISTORY'

Does he think wealth ever affects people's opinions? 'Well, yes, I'm a Marxist, after all.' So why would his own opinions be mysteriously immune to his bank balance? 'Well, because I can't trace any connection.' Doesn't he find that unusual? He pauses to consider. 'Well, no, because I think that comes in with inherited wealth.'

– Decca Aitkenhead, 'Christopher Hitchens'

What impression did Hitchens's revolutionary phase leave on his politics? He always claimed to be a Marxist. When he was interviewed in

2007, before the credit crunch, Hitchens was asked about the role of neoliberal capitalism in driving US wars and whether this did not have its own injustices. He acknowledged the point but suggested that 'there appears to be' a connection between a free market and a free society and that the promulgation of a liberal policy would in many parts of the world 'be a step up'.

Since capitalism no longer faced an 'ideological enemy' with 'a plausible theory of power', it was

> reasserting itself as the only revolution. And it takes a Marxist to see it, sometimes ... Joseph Schumpeter called it creative destruction: capitalism needs to go on devouring things and making things unstable and dangerous in order to keep on existing. Finding shorter and more scientific routes to production, productivity, demand, efficiency, discarding waste or competition, creating and then breaking up monopolies. It creates a destructive force. But anyone can recognize it as a revolution. It's the only revolution in town.[57]

This is the context in which to interpret Hitchens's claim that the American revolution is the only one left standing.

So, despite ceasing to be involved in any form of socialist politics, and indeed despite actively championing a 'Jeffersonian' (neoliberal) imperialism, Hitchens did not cease calling himself a Marxist. Given his statements about capitalism, it is fair to say this Marxism failed to give him the foresight to see that the immanent tendencies of the world system were heralding catastrophe. Still, when the credit crunch occurred, Hitchens was alert to capitalism's self-consummation. In *Hitch-22* he wrote:

> As I sat down to set this down, having done somewhat better out of capitalism than I had ever expected to do, the financial markets had just crashed on almost the precise day on which I became fifty-nine and one-half years of age, and thus eligible to make use of my Wall Street–managed 'retirement fund'. My old Marxism came back to me as I contemplated the 'dead labour' that had been hoarded in that account, saw it being squandered in a victory for finance capital over industrial capital, noticed the ancient dichotomy between use value and exchange value, and saw again the victory of those monopolists who 'make' money over those who only have the power to earn it.[58]

Indeed, as the recession did its worst, and some flashes of resistance foreshadowing the Occupy movement broke through, he could be found eulogising the radical traditions of Wisconsin (that ouvrieriste strain) and censuring the banks and the Bush administration.[59] Mugged by reality he may have been, this display seemed to signal, but he had been left with the rudiments of his critical faculties intact. Far from joining the serried lines of neoconservatives fawning over the executive and screeching for the murder of Arabs, Hitchens retained a Marxist analytic that sharpened his insights to the last.

Yet Hitchens had not merely abandoned the moral commitment at the centre of Marxism. He had decided that the very conditions that made Marxism intelligible as a form of analysis no longer existed. Hitchens had said, explaining his abandonment of socialism:

> Is there now an international working-class movement that has a feasible idea for a better society? No, there isn't. Will it revive? The answer is clearly no. Is there a socialist critique of the capitalist world order? No. Realizing that, to call myself a socialist would be a sentimental thing.[60]

This indeed grasps something essential to the Marxist case. If the main form of antagonism in society is class antagonism, then the prospects for socialism rest on the ability of a working-class movement to confront and replace capitalism. But in the case of the disappearance of that prospect, Marxism must be considered defunct as well. Pretending otherwise would be sentimental under such circumstances.

More important, a version of the use-mention problem arises here. At various stages in his career Hitchens meant different things by the term *Marxism*, and this by no means coincided with what might be called a routine understanding of Marxism. Hitchens had a tendency to bowdlerise the theoretical issues that he delved into, perhaps in part because of a writer's urge to simplify. But this had more than an element of simple philistinism and a thin line between oversimplification and travesty. Thus, for example, defending Anglo-Saxon theory from the depredations of postmodernists and continentals, he suggested that postmodernism could be defined as 'the view that nothing would ever again happen for the first time' and Louis Althusser's political philosophy as an 'attempt to recreate Communism by abstract thought'.[61]

Some of the elements of Hitchens's vulgarisation of Marxism were apparent in his earlier works. Hitchens tended to mean three kinds of things when he used the term *Marxism*. Of these the most persistent was a simplistic, progressivist view of historical development. This is particularly apparent in his writings on Marxism and empire, as well as his celebration of the US conquest of the Native Americans. But it is also evident in the declaration that the truly revolutionary thing to do in the current era was to align with neoliberal capitalism and in his taunting suggestion that Halliburton had as much right as anyone else to take over Iraq's oil (since Iraqis plainly could not be trusted with it themselves).[62] The second was a crude materialism that had a tendency to flip over into idealism. This was apparent in almost all his writings on religion, wherein he treated religious ideas not as a complex lived relationship of human beings to their situation but rather as a simple fantasy. The third, perhaps surprisingly, was a meritocratic ideology.

To explain. In an interview with Decca Aitkenhead of the *Guardian* of London, Hitchens was asked why, if he acknowledged that a person's ideology was at least partially determined by class, he could not allow that his own soaring bank balance partially determined his ideology. In reply he excluded his bank balance as a factor on the ground that it was not inherited wealth.

To say that this misstates the Marxist conception of the relationship between class and ideology would be to miss the point. What Hitchens was surreptitiously offering here was an understanding of class as a set of relative market advantages and political privileges transmitted from generation to generation by the mechanism of inheritance. Wealth accumulated in one's own lifetime, in contrast, would be extraneous to any determination of class. If wealth is not the result of nepotism, monopoly, or political dynasty, it must reflect only talent and hard work. This is the myth of the self-made man, a myth whose repressed truth is the cooperative labour of many. (In Hitchens's case the return of the repressed would occur each time someone spotted one of his many plagiarisms or demanded credit for their work.) When Hitchens complained of the 'dead labour' squandered in the stock market crash, he referred of course to what he took to be *his* dead labour. This was the vein in which he reproved the victory of monopolists who make money over those who earn it.[63]

It is not difficult to see Hitchens's rediscovery of Marxism as a form of whining about his own lost earnings. In this light we can assume that his outrage was absolutely genuine and, as always, personal. The importance of Marxism to Hitchens after his apostasy was thus largely sentimental and psychological. Hitchens continually returned to the themes of historical materialism at least in part to demonstrate his fidelity and the left's corruption, as well as to scratch an old itch. This tendency had been particularly evident in the earliest phase of his apostasy, but its return to the fore as the crisis of global capitalism ate into his retirement funds is perhaps a testament to the old Marxist saw about the determination of ideology by material circumstance.

2 ENGLISH QUESTIONS, FROM ORWELL TO THATCHER

Many is the honourable radical and revolutionary who may be found in the camp of the apparent counterrevolution. And the radical conservative is not a contradiction in terms.

— Christopher Hitchens, *Letters to a Young Contrarian*

It took me years to admit it to anybody, but when the election day came I deliberately did not vote to keep Labour in office. I had various private excuses … But in truth, I secretly knew quite well that I wasn't merely registering an abstention. I was in effect voting for Mrs Thatcher. And I was secretly, guiltily glad to see her terminating the long reign of mediocrity and torpor.

— Christopher Hitchens, *Hitch-22*

ENGLISH QUESTIONS 1: MRS THATCHER

ROBERT NOVAK: You don't condone this [poll tax] rioting, do you, Mr Hitchens?
CHRISTOPHER HITCHENS: I always welcome signs of confrontation.

— CNN, 1990

Precisely what it was about Mrs Thatcher's femininity that attracted Hitchens is not entirely clear from his multiple accounts of the concupiscence. His hyperventilating eulogies to the adamantine leader of British reaction usually took as their point of departure a brief encounter between the pair which resulted in his being lightly spanked with 'a rolled-up parliamentary order paper' and adjudged a 'naughty boy'. He had written of the romantic poet Byron that he was 'intimately aware of the relationship between sex and cruelty'. It is fair to say that Hitchens was too, as the sadism–masochism couplet frequently made an appearance in his writing. And if he wrote of sado-masochism primarily as a relation between ruler and ruled to be deplored and resisted, it clearly also had its temptations.

Another term that entered Hitchens's lexicon was *sado-monetarism*, epitomising the Thatcher government's aggressive assault on welfare and wages in the name of counterinflation. Knowing of Hitchens's relief at her election, and the end of, as he put it, the torpor, mediocrity, and 'tax-funded statism' that her ascension signified, it may not be stretching the point to say that he could see the bright side of the sadistic whipping into line of a resilient social democratic consensus by an obdurate neo-liberal leadership.[1]

The term *sado-monetarism*, coined by Denis Healey (perhaps to distinguish Thatcher's monetarism from his own softer variety), was by no means merely facetious. It grasped something essential to Thatcherism. As Stuart Hall argued, Thatcher spoke to something

> deep in the English psyche: its masochism. The need which the English seem to have to be ticked off by Nanny and sent to bed without a pudding. The calculus by which every good summer has to be paid for by twenty bad winters. The Dunkirk Spirit – the worse off we are, the better we behave. She didn't promise us the give-away society. She said, iron times; back to the wall; stiff upper lip; get moving; get to work; dig in. Stick by the old, tried verities, the wisdom of 'Old England'. The family has kept society together; live by it. Send the women back to the hearth. Get the men out on to the Northwest Frontier. Hard times – followed, much later, by a return to the Good Old Days. She asked you for a long leash – not one, but two and three terms. By the end, she said, I will be able to redefine the nation in such a way that you will all, once again, for the first time, since the Empire started to go down the tube, feel what it is like to be part of Great Britain Unlimited. You will be able, once again, to send our boys 'over there', to fly the flag, to welcome back the fleet. Britain will be Great again.[2]

Through such thematics Thatcherism translated

> economic doctrine into the language of experience, moral imperative and common sense … an alternative ethic to that of the 'caring society'. This translation of a theoretical ideology into a populist idiom was a major political achievement: and the conversion of hard-faced economics into the language of compulsive moralism was, in many ways, the

centrepiece of this transformation … This assault, not just on welfare over-spending but on the very principle and ethic of collective social welfare … was mounted, not through an analysis of which class of the deserving made most out of the welfare state, but through the emotive language of the 'scrounger': the new folk-devil.[3]

It would be churlish, then, to deny Hitchens's insight into the basis of Thatcherism, including his visceral understanding of – as he put it – the 'literal-minded John Bullshit' that he had 'spent years' arguing himself out of, not to mention the Churchillian bluster that he found on the American right during Desert Storm. And it is understandable that he should be so vexed by the left's apparent lack of comprehension, condemning itself 'to experiencing major phenomena – the Falklands fever; Mrs Thatcher herself – as a surprise'. Certainly, Hitchens had a point about the conservative, squalid nature of the postwar compromise (particularly in the phase of high decadence it had reached by the 1970s), and in saying that if the left could not revolutionise that state of affairs as it ground to miserable stagnation, then the task would 'fall to the Right'. It is simply that this insight cannot be dissociated from 'the rodent slowly stirring' in his 'viscera: the uneasy but unbanishable feeling that on some essential matters [Thatcher] might be right'.[4]

It must be said, however, that whatever Hitchens was to claim in later years, he gave few on the left any indication whatever of any concord with Thatcherism at the time. His writing was, if anything, uncompromisingly anti-Tory. His early report on the Tories' 1979 victory had no edge of Thatcher fancying. On the contrary, it confirmed everything he disliked about old England:

> Edmund Wilson would not have had to alter his description, in 1945, of basic English qualities: 'The passion for social privilege, the rapacious appetite for property, the egoism that damns one's neighbour, the dependence on inherited advantages and the almost equally deep-fibred instinct, often not deliberate or conscious, to make all these appear forms of virtue.'[5]

And in fact, far from expecting the Thatcherites to revolutionise stale Britannia, he gloated at the U-turns of the government, noted the failure of its policies with satisfaction, and warned:

> Thatcher cannot govern forever by a mixture of the dole-queue and 'Rule Britannia'. Still, her education is proving an expensive one – pace

Lady Bracknell – for the rest of us to finance. Other nations tempted to succumb to neoconservative blandishments should study the British experience of what Robert Lowell once called, in another connection, 'the reign of piety and iron'.[6]

Upon Thatcher's downfall Hitchens reflected that she had been 'a radical and not a reactionary'. Later Hitchens deemed her to be both 'Britain's most reactionary' and most revolutionary prime minister – a much more typically Hitchensian formulation. She had 'made possible a movement for a serious, law-based constitutional republic in Britain' and 'hacked away at the encrusted institutions and attitudes that stood in its path'.[7] He thus hinted, at least before his explicit endorsement of Thatcher in 2001, that it was not merely her tender spank that aroused Hitchens's amour but the Thatcherite modernisation project in toto. But this was arguably a slip and not one in which he fully disclosed his ambivalent support for Thatcher.

Even on the question of 'the Falklands fever' and Britain's imperial past, which evidently caused Hitchens's instinctive Thatcherism to kick out most forcefully, he wrote nothing favourable to Thatcher at the time and did not trumpet his prowar sentiment widely. 'If Christopher had ever said a good word about Margaret Thatcher,' D. D. Guttenplan recalled,

I'd have noticed it, because nobody did. I remember reading his book and thinking about what he said about the Falklands, and I went back to see whether there was any printed evidence of him ever saying anything pro-Thatcherite. I'm not saying it doesn't exist, but I looked pretty hard, and I couldn't find anything.[8]

Nonetheless, Amy Wilentz, another *Nation* journalist who knew Hitchens well, recounts that he did in fact disclose his sympathy for Thatcher in that conflict to her. 'As he got older,' Wilentz suggests,

the sturdy, British character of his father, a former naval commander known to all Christopher's friends as the Commander, began to assert itself in Christopher's personality. This was the side of him that, again, to my political shock, supported the queen (to say nothing of Margaret Thatcher, then reviled by all good left-leaning Britons) in the matter of the Falkland Islands. I remember him gathering himself up grandly in the Cafe Loup near The Nation (a bistro he referred to as simply, the Loo) and telling me he would happily serve on one of her majesty's ships that were at that moment steaming toward the waters off Argentina to keep the sheep and shepherds safely under British rule. Christopher turned out to be a patriot. Weird.[9]

So when the military dictatorship of Argentina led by General Galtieri invaded the Falkland Islands, a colonial possession populated by British subjects, Hitchens was indeed among those to demand retribution. 'I couldn't possibly see the UK defeated by those insanitary riffraff!' he later said. 'This was a diabolical liberty.' The left gloss that he put on this position was that the defeat of the Argentinian forces would pre-cipitate the downfall of Galtieri, whom he characterised as a fascist. He also drew a connection to Washington's policy of supporting death squads and dictatorships in the hemisphere, depicting Thatcher's war as a breach with the Reaganites.[10]

In one sense Hitchens was proved right. Galtieri was indeed stripped of his post by the Argentinian military after an inquiry into the strategic and tactical failures of the war. Apart from anything else, the war pushed the regime into economic turmoil, as its debts were underwritten by UK banks. The political calculation that a bloodless invasion would give Argentina a strong bargaining chip for negotiating the return of the Malvinas, and that the US would either remain neutral or intervene on Argentina's side with Mrs Thatcher, was wildly mistaken. The junta, already divided over a range of problems, including the question of how far to implement the neoliberal policies pioneered by the Chilean regime, was undoubtedly further weakened and divided by the defeat. This hastened the subsequent transition to civilian rule.[11]

In reality, however, the fall of Galtieri was a by-product of something that Hitchens wanted more, the reassertion of British power, particu-larly of its naval power. Moreover, it is not as if regimes fall only when defeated from without. Certainly, Galtieri's political demise might have been slower had the Thatcher regime negotiated some pragmatic settlement with the Argentinian government. But the regime was hardly a stable or popular one.

It is important to stress the morbid effects of the Falklands War on British political culture at the time. If, to his American friends, Hitchens's reaction was simply idiosyncratic, it was not necessarily so in the UK context. One can argue that any long-range effect of the war on British culture is superfluous, but the nationalist suppuration at the time was potent, symbolised by the defiant revival of the bunting and the old imperialist warble 'Rule Britannia'. The invasion of the Falklands had acted with force on the ongoing sensation of national decline and malaise. The postwar sense of social peace had been shattered. Orwell had evoked 'the deep, deep sleep of England' in the prewar era, and the dominant ideology in postwar England had been just as soporific. As Anthony Barnett had put it:

> A classless sense of 'fair-play' was seen to preside over social relations within the UK. All loved the Queen, and the amusing antique ceremonies of monarchy thus unified classes and regions. The quiet sense of shared self-confidence was conjured up by the unarmed 'bobby'; the police were like uncles who kept a kindly eye out for understandable misdemeanours, crimes of passion and the very infrequent villain. There was no country like it.[12]

This social imaginary, through which large numbers of people sometimes lived their relationship to their social conditions, was not merely an idle idyll. Nationalist language, with all its vagueness, does indirectly allude to the material modes of existence of polyglot social layers – retaining its ability to do so precisely through its indirectness. As such it must somehow represent aspects of real life, even as it misrepresents them. The stability of British society – which Hitchens valued as the 'splendid and unique privilege of traceable, stable community' – was compounded because, unlike almost every major European society, it had not suffered occupation, conquest, civil war, or revolution by the time of the Second World War.[13] Class antagonisms were not superseded but allayed by the relative health and stability of the postwar system. The corporatist mode of governance, through which trade unions were incorporated, along with employers, into national agreements about wages and conditions, also provided a material substratum for the notion of fair play. The monarchy did reestablish its credibility after the debacle of Edward VIII's abdication and flirtation with fascism. The police hardly conformed to the *Dixon of Dock Green* stereotype, but many people believed that they did.[14]

This social image was reduced to a spectral form, however, when the conditions of postwar peace disintegrated. And it was connotatively linked to another sensation of loss, that of the colonies. National identity, as with other identities, is relational, dependent on its situation vis-á-vis Others. Britishness was historically defined first in its imperial capacity, because the union of the Kingdom of England and the

Kingdom of Scotland symbolised the consolidated strategic base from which two aggressive colonial powers could make an undivided bid for world power. Together, Perfidious Albion and Imperial Caledonia set out to create a new world order. Linda Colley makes the case that British identity was decisively formed through Britain's imperialist extensions into the Americas, Africa and South Asia, and its encounters with various Others.[15] Empire had provided the moral and historical mission that had defined Britishness, particularly in the high colonial era beginning in the late nineteenth century. The 'end of empire' elegies captured the tremendous sadness on the right at the end of this purpose, but the sense of a crisis of Britannia was much more widespread. And despite the creative energies unleashed by the radicalisation of the early 1970s, the mounting social crisis, stagflation, and an increasingly violent society enabled the right to articulate a racialised 'law and order' response to the crisis. As Hitchens had rightly guessed, the inability of the forces of the left to impose their own solution to this malaise would open the opportunity for the hard right. This was where Thatcherism had come in. But the early years of Thatcher's administration had, as Hitchens noted, only exacerbated the crisis. The Falklands invasion had acted on this, producing an ideal opportunity structure for someone like Thatcher to offer iron leadership.

This perhaps puts Hitchens's sense of social democratic nadir and stagnation in a new perspective. It is not difficult to detect in his weariness about the drab littleness of postwar Britain those melancholic feelings associated with the passing of fantasies of imperial omnipotence. As he put it in an elegiac moment, after the Suez debacle 'the tide of empire and dominion merely and sadly ebbed.' This 'postcolonial melancholia', as Paul Gilroy has dubbed it, has never brought out the best in anyone, and its effects can be detected in the very worst of Hitchens, as in his writing about 'Londonistan'.[16]

There is a tradition of racist English witticism by which, not to put too fine a point on it, a place is raced. Someone cheerfully bristling with contempt for immigrants is apt to inform one that such and such a town might as well be known as New Delhi, Mogadishu, or other more inventive and less delightful place names. To the same family of satirical levity belongs the old anti-Semitic trope that dubs New York 'Jew York'; likewise, the *New York Times* the 'Jew York Times'. Now we might add 'Eurabia', used by the far right academic Bat Ye'or to describe a pro-Arab conspiracy of European elites. And *Londonistan*, which refers to the supposed infiltration by 'radical Islam' of the city's communities and institutions, performs a similar function. In this view the London of Routemasters, St Stephen's Tower, the Thames, and the redoubtable cabbie has acquired an unwelcome Islamic hue and cry.

In a 2007 article titled 'Londonistan Calling', with a subheading that asked how a nation moved 'from cricket and fish-and-chips to burkas and shoe-bombers in a single generation', Hitchens described the fate of a North London town under the influence of 'radical Islam':

> In my lost youth I lived in Finsbury Park, a shabby area of North London, roughly between the old Arsenal football ground and the Seven Sisters Road. It was a working-class neighborhood, with a good number of Irish and Cypriot immigrants. Your food choices were the inevitable fish-and-chips, plus the curry joint, plus a strong pitch from the Greek and Turkish kebab sellers …
>
> Returning to the old place after a long absence, I found that it was the scent of Algeria that now predominated along the main thoroughfare of Blackstock Road. This had had a good effect on the quality of the coffee and the spiciness of the grocery stores. But it felt odd, under the gray skies of London, to see women wearing the veil, and even swathed in the chador or the all-enveloping burka. Many of these Algerians, Bangladeshis, and others are also refugees from conflict in their own country. Indeed, they have often been the losers in battles against Middle Eastern and Asian regimes which they regard as insufficiently Islamic. Quite unlike the Irish and the Cypriots, they bring these far-off quarrels along with them. And they also bring a religion which is not ashamed to speak of conquest and violence.[17]

Hitchens had not chosen to visit the London towns with the highest Muslim populations. His panic may have overwhelmed him if, instead of Finsbury Park (which has a Muslim population of less than 12 per cent), he had visited Bethnal Green (where slightly less than half the population are Bangladeshi Muslims), Whitechapel (where more than half are Bangladeshi Muslims), or other redoubts of Tower Hamlets. The sole reason for alighting on Finsbury Park was the connection with a would-be 'shoe-bomber' who had attended unofficial sermons at a local mosque – and because of the way the popular press in the UK had used this as an audit of the state of Islam.[18]

At any rate, having chosen Finsbury Park for his own balance sheet of British Islam, he did not bother himself with the real dilemmas or daily experiences of his subjects. This was hardly *The Road to Seven Sisters*.

Instead, he followed the vast majority of the British media in identifying the tiny cluster of jihadis in Britain as an existential threat – a serious challenge for the ownership of Britain. Moreover, he did his utmost to connect their activities to the beliefs of the wider Muslim cohort. His point, that the Muslims were doing England down, was comprehensible mainly in the light of his wider understanding of British decline.

Hitchens was a native and partisan of an England that existed only for some and only for some of the time. It was in fact a highly aleatory England, a chance conjunction of various colonial dependencies, including Malta, with maritime Portsmouth; prep school in Devon; public school in Cambridge; Balliol College, Oxford; Bloomsbury; and the media circuits in London. Added to these typical upper-middle-class milieus were the Labour Party and the International Socialists, a 'small but growing post-Trotskyist Luxemburgist sect', as he was to inaccurately describe it. So, in addition to befriending Martin Amis, being within the circumference of A. J. Ayers, bedding future Thatcherite cabinet ministers, and meeting 'senior ministers and parliamentarians "up close"', he came to know Peter Sedgwick, and C. L. R. James, to have Christopher Hill as his head of college, and to be in the orbit of Michael Rosen and Tariq Ali. The revolutionary filiations of Hitchens in this period were hardly insincere, but they seem to have coexisted with an unspoken feeling for an England that had passed away. And as he lost the revolutionary faith, a part of him saw in Thatcherism an authentic force for renewal.

ENGLISH QUESTIONS 2: WRITERS IN THE EMPIRE

RICHARD CRITCHLEY: I spent, oh, twenty years or so living in the Third World. And I find the after-effect of empire ... practically all to the good. It's amazing. One time I was in Sudan ... and a cattle thief was being tried, and he said, 'You can't try me, I'm from another tribe,' and the judge held up this pathetic, tattered old law book, it was the English colonial law, saying, 'The law is the law no matter where.' And then once in Dhaka, I was in a riot, and my Bengali interpreter, he was kind of aghast at what was happening, turned to me, and he said, 'My father read Macaulay and he wore a suit and tie every day of his life.' In other words, the sun really hasn't set.
CHRISTOPHER HITCHENS: I must say both of your stories make one proud to be British, and I think there are some good legacies to it. Notably of course the English language, which I think is a great international language.

– C-SPAN, 18 June 1990

The 'beloved canon of English writing' was, for Hitchens, almost unimpeachable. By far the most heartfelt benediction he could bestow on anyone, be it C. L. R. James or Edward Said, was that they were literate in the canon. James

> had schooled himself in classical literature and regarded the canon of English as something with which every literate person of any culture should become acquainted ... This commitment was important then and was to become much more so as the 1960s fashion turned against 'Eurocentrism'.

Likewise, 'when Edward talked about English literature and quoted from it, he passed the test that I always privately apply: Do you truly love this subject and could you bear to live for one moment if it was obliterated?'[19]

The taint Hitchens could least bear was any whiff of 'atonal postmodernism', deconstruction, Third Worldism, or 'negritude'. These modes of criticism, with their decidedly non-Anglo inflections and alienating languages of abstraction, appalled Hitchens. Like many an offspring of the English middle class, he was deeply suspicious of such conceptual conceits and their distance from visceral experience. But above all he was unwilling to tolerate the erosion of prestige that such criticism inflicted on the canon or at least on the conception of Western culture as, in the words of Robert Scholes, 'a single coherent object, constructed of masterpieces built by geniuses'.[20]

At times Hitchens fancied that the Anglo-American idiom could be 'a world language ... without being an imperial one ... the first to the extent that it has ceased to be the second'.[21] This was a mirage, however, and as he demonstrated in his C-Span conversation with Richard Critchley, Hitchens was well aware of the entanglement of the worldwide propagation of English with imperialism – indeed, it was one of the points in favour of empire. Where Hitchens may have had a point is that so far as it was bound up with empire, the ascendancy of English was coextensive with the increasing parochialism of English culture, what Franco Moretti considers a cultural autarky. The more expansive England's dominion, the more worldly experience it incorporated, the less it had reference to other cultural formations, and, to that extent, the less worldly it became.[22]

Of course, just as the English ruling class was enriched by the appropriated labour of its colonial subjects, so its culture was always replenished by their work. The literary critic Terry Eagleton once remarked on how fortunate the English were that the Irish had written some of their best literature for them. Equally, England's global power included sufficient cultural allure to attract talented foreigners. But in the modern era a consequence of the destruction of colonial rule was that African and Indian writers forced their way into the canon of English literature. As Jonah Raskin put it in the 1970s:

> Modern British literature was created by Irishmen, Americans, and a Pole. Outstanding contemporary literature in English is more and more the product of Africans and Indians – Wole Soyinka, R. K. Narayan, V. S. Naipaul. Modern British culture colonized writers from varied cultures and national backgrounds.[23]

Indeed, the expansive character and parochial universalism of the English canon was precisely what made Hitchens one of its most determined defenders. As an English provincial from a military family, he had a particular fondness for empire literature – Paul Scott's *The Raj Quartet*, Kipling's *Kim*, or 'The White Man's Burden', George Macdonald Fraser's *Flashman* narratives or, to a lesser extent, the more disturbing work of Conrad.[24] Hitchens also had a propensity for defending 'politically incorrect' authors against their left-wing critics, be it Paul Scott against Salman Rushdie, or Philip Larkin against John Newsinger.

It was not always a question of baiting the left. Hitchens sincerely appreciated the critical, subversive energies that could coexist with racist, authoritarian, or fascist ideologies in literary works (rather, he saw that they could come from the same experiential sources), as well as the wrenching ambiguities the authors of such literature could inhabit. One of his late review essays about Saki, a far right satirist whose life was extinguished in the Great War, alighted on the contradictions of the author's personality, centred on the question of empire: 'His affectless poseurs and dandies may have reflected one half of the man … But this other hemisphere of his character also admired wildness and risk and cruelty and warfare, and associated the concepts of empire and nation with manly virtue.'

By 1914 Saki 'appeared to forget all his previous affectations about hollandaise dressing and the loving preparations of wine and cheese' and signed up for the trenches. The louche affectation and rococo composition gave way to Mainwaringesque reaction. But Hitchens saw in this transition something faintly admirable, in that Saki 'had finally come to decide that other people were worth fighting for after all'.[25] Hitchens well knew that these 'other people' were merely the English gentry, that Saki's was a narcissistic solidarity with 'people like me'. Yet at this stage (the essay was published in 2008), the contradiction that Saki lived and the way he finally resolved it bore sufficient similarities to Hitchens's own psychic progress as to perhaps soften the reviewer's judgement.

Among the empire's scribes, it was the 'bard of empires', Rudyard Kipling, who 'not only captured the spirit of imperialism and the white man's burden but also wrote imperishable stories and poems'.[26] Aside from Kipling's 'permanent contradictions', for Hitchens one of the most compelling things about Kipling was his Anglo-Americanism. Hitchens always viewed it as an advantage if an English writer had some relationship to America. One of his few real criticisms of Orwell was that the latter did not really like the United States, and indeed one of the few censorious moments in Hitchens's discussion of Kipling is when he describes in a disapproving tone the poet's dislike of Americans. Nonetheless, Kipling had lived in the United States, married an American woman, and wrote of the white man's burden as a beseeching overture to the United States of America on the occasion of the Spanish-American War. This was a key literary moment in the fabled Anglophone imperial succession, which *Blood, Class, and Nostalgia* took as its subject.

Kipling had sent his poem to the 'Rough Rider' and alpha imperialist Theodore Roosevelt, and he and Henry Cabot Lodge had used lines from 'The White Man's Burden' in support of the colonial turn in which the US took possession of Spain's former possessions, including the Philippines, a key base from which to begin the penetration of China. By encouraging the imperialist faction of US politics, Kipling's goal was to draft America's enviable dynamism and power onto the British side in world affairs. His influence was immense, a 'Kipling Boom' that coincided with America's debut in overseas colonialism. 'The White Man's Burden' was endlessly recapitulated and parodied, as well as mined for its cadences. Later Kipling was a key lobbyist for American entry into World War I, fulminating about the threat of Prussian barbarism, scalding about early Wilsonian neutrality, and contemptuous of his postwar agenda for peace. And Hitchens retraced elements of Kipling's postmortem role as a source of propaganda and imperialist ideology in the United States, until FDR cannily seized his moment to claim global dominion.[27]

The tone of Hitchens's narrative was critical and vaguely satirical, but a hermeneutical reading of it must start from his own avowed attitude towards empire. He consistently argued (and I return to this later in the chapter) that the British Empire was a necessary, if brutal, phase in the development of otherwise feudal and reactionary societies. It was a relatively progressive development. Likewise, he would argue that 1492 was 'a very good year' and that the ensuing process of colonisation and extermination should be celebrated on the basis of the progress wrought in its wake.[28]

It would be too much to claim that Hitchens approved of Kipling's sentiment, or of the American conquest of the Philippines, though he may well have thought it ultimately a progressive development; far less so Kipling's work in arousing the fervour for American entry into World War I. When Hitchens wrote this book, he was still capable of being bitterly critical of the crimes of imperialism. But there are symptomatic silences where one might expect context. For example, that he left unexplored the bitter human costs of the colonisation may have been predictable, given Hitchens's conception of progress, and of indigenous life as so much raw material for that end. But Hitchens did not even weigh the regressive impact on the US, in terms of the relationship between militarism, conquest, and the bolstering of white supremacy internally. And this, given Kipling's emphasis on the confraternity of Anglo-America through a (presumed) shared whiteness, can be considered a serious omission.

In addition, Hitchens's cheering of Kipling's ability to sum up the spirit of the white man's burden contained a notable lack of caution, (he did not place the phrase in scare quotes). This is not to say that Hitchens would have subscribed to the racial epithets, but he did believe in this burden in a sense and not only in his later years as a Jeffersonian imperialist – even if he was sceptical of the role that the notion of a burden played in imperialist psychology. When he wrote in 2002 that Kipling 'believed that the barbarians were always mustering on the frontier, and that order and good government could be maintained only by a stoic, disciplined, self-conscious, and self-sacrificing minority', Hitchens's tone held no trace of irony. Yet by this point he had publicly taken up battle against the barbarians and was very much aligned with the disciplined minority he considered corevolutionists. Like Kipling, he had little interest in empire as 'an economic system' and regretted the insularity of culture in the metropole, worrying that this lack of international consciousness would lose America its awesome dominion.[29]

Yet, aside from the urgency of Kipling's appeal to the United States, there is another tone in 'The White Man's Burden', in the starkness of his contrasts and the heaviness of his ironies – a sad, wistful sense of empire's imminent decline, that the forces of lawlessness will prevail over the cultured hierarchy of the colonies. The refrain 'Take up the white man's burden' itself appears as simultaneously imperative and weary – and increasingly the latter as the poem goes on.[30] And this historical experience of decline, and Kipling's rendering of it, stirred Hitchens:

> To those born or brought up in England after 1914, let alone 1945, the sense of a waning day is part of the assumed historical outcome. It was Kipling's achievement to have sounded this sad, admonishing note during the imperial midday, and to have conveyed the premonition among his hearers that dusk was nearer than they had thought.[31]

This 'postcolonial melancholia' is inescapably present in another of Hitchens's favourite writers, Philip Larkin. By no means an exoteric imperialist like Kipling, he 'was an artist and he was a thwarted fascist'. He did nonetheless come to signify a certain idea of England, bound up with the empire, and in his poetry as in his life he did regret the decline of the British Empire. 'Homage to a Government', Larkin's lament on the retreat from Aden, is a classic of this form. Even if it contains 'no element of vulgar intolerance', as Hitchens insisted, and does largely stick to the theme that Labour's small-minded penny-pinching had cost England its national greatness, there is a jarring moment for an informed reader. 'It's hard to say who wanted it to happen', the poem muses. This is not strictly serious. The author would have known that those who wanted it to happen were the inhabitants of the places the soldiers 'guarded, or kept orderly'. But the line directs attention to a structuring absence in the verses, their inability to see these places as real, historical entities, their inhabitants as the agents willing and bringing about this end. It is not vulgar intolerance but colonial indifference and contempt expressed here. And, contra Hitchens, 'Homage to a Government' was not unique in Larkin's published oeuvre in expressing his 'resentful conservatism'.

'Going, Going', a poem whose impressionistic merits Hitchens sought to defend, alongside its political insight, was a classic expression of the resentful, axe-grinding, declensionism of the postwar right. 'And that will be England gone / The shadows, the meadows, the lanes' may have reproved the speculators ('spectacled grins') who profited from land, but it also rebuked the kids 'screaming for more / More houses, more parking allowed, / More caravan sites, more pay'. And it reviled the growing population that brought with it such demands, threatening to reduce England to the 'First slum in Europe'. It was, then, a complaint against modernity, against development, and against population growth, from the right. The poem which, for Hitchens, 'captured the England of Heath and Slater-Walker too well', was entirely consistent and resonant with the verse Larkin wrote to his lover Monica Jones, complaining that England had 'welcomed in the scum, / First of Europe, then the world'.

Hitchens rejected the vicious racism of this latter verse, but in defending 'Going, Going' as he did, in such an undifferentiating fashion, he showed that the axe grinding and resentment were his, too. Even if he admired and appreciated the critical perspicacity of Larkin the artist, aspects of the weltanschauung of Larkin the 'thwarted fascist' also resonated with Hitchens. This is not to say that Hitchens simply embraced this reactionary melancholia – as ever, he preferred a certain degree of ambiguity. But it formed an aspect of his own personality. As he explained,

> I have never had any difficulty comprehending the appeal of Larkin to some part of the British (not so much the English) consciousness. This is because I recall, with very little trouble, the tone of my own father's table talk.

Hitchens understood the 'Poujadiste' mentality that arose in part from the social misery of the functionary class in the interwar generation, forming around the issues of imperial decline and Commonwealth immigration and extending to dysphoria over the ravages to countryside and moral conduct. He did not openly embrace it, but it is symptomatic that in disclosing this side of his own socialisation, he felt impelled to mention 'the Falklands fever' as an expression of such pessimistic chauvinism – but did not mention his own surrender to that fever, which he never recanted.[32]

ENGLISH QUESTIONS 3: ORWELL

No writer was as persistent in the defence of George Orwell, and the prosecution of his critics and would-be appropriators on the right, than Christopher Hitchens. This was the stuff of controversy in the *Nation* magazine, where his colleague Alexander Cockburn savaged Orwell as a snitch and bully in light of the well-known list of names that the author passed, in his dying days, to Celia Kirwan of the Information Research Department. This list was to be used by the IRD, a propaganda apparatus of the British state, to ensure that the government did not hire the wrong sort of person. While Hitchens had rashly claimed that 'Orwell named no names and disclosed no identities', Cockburn charged that Orwell's supporters were rationalising a witch-hunt over loyalty and noted how they tended 'to skate gently over Orwell's suspicions of Jews, homosexuals and blacks, also over the extreme ignorance of his assessments'.[33]

The significance of this list has been exaggerated in many ways. Orwell was ill and in love with Kirwan. And, while Cockburn points out the IRD's role in forming alliances with Ukrainian nationalists, Orwell seems to have been ignorant of the IRD's true role, believing it to be simply defending the case for social democracy against both Stalinism and the right. Moreover, Orwell's actions at times belied any suggestion of McCarthyite sympathies on his part. For example, he protested the ten-year prison sentence given to Alan Nunn May, a scientist who had passed nuclear information to the USSR. Hitchens is also correct to say that, unlike in the United States, the pro-Soviet attitudes that Orwell thought he was countering were by no means those of a beleaguered minority but quite respectable in large parts of the left.[34]

Yet in several other respects Hitchens's defence of Orwell on this question is simply untenable. First, note his strategies of minimisation. Hitchens implied there was no revelation. The list had already been published, hence there was nothing new to talk about. In fact, what had actually happened was that Bernard Crick had once alluded to the list in a biography of Orwell. In fact, the context would not have allowed readers to understand its significance. An official biography published in 1991 had erroneously described the list as serving primarily to satisfy Orwell's own curiosity. It was not until the 1996 completion of Peter Davison's twenty volumes of the collected Orwell, which included the author's notebooks, that the full context was disclosed. Only then was it clear that the list was an effort on behalf of the British state. Further, Hitchens rebuffed claims that the list was in any sense a blacklist: a 'blacklist is a roster of names maintained by those with the power to affect hiring and firing'.[35] But that was precisely the purpose of the list: to identify Communists and their sympathisers and to ensure that they were not employed.

In *Orwell's Victory* Hitchens made much of the few examples of Orwell's having named a secret sympathiser with the USSR, and the one example of his having identified an actual Soviet agent. Peter Smollett, who had worked in the Ministry of Information, was conclusively proved to be 'an agent of Soviet security; this represents a match of

100 per cent between Orwell's allegation of direct foreign recruitment and the known facts.'[36] Yet, if the aim was to prevent potential saboteurs from being employed by a government propaganda service, it is surely striking that from an initial list of 135 suspects, and a narrower list of thirty-five suspects, only one was actually in the pay of the USSR. Everyone else was at most a sympathiser and generally charged on the basis of insinuation or guilt by association.

Most of those on Orwell's list were simply people on the left who, for one reason or another, Orwell distrusted and disliked. Even less convincing was the effort that Hitchens made to acquit Orwell of the charge of racism arising from comments he made in the list. 'Some critics,' Hitchens submitted, 'notably Frances Stonor Saunders in her book *Who Paid The Piper?*, have allowed a delicate wrinkling of the nostril at Orwell's inclusion of details about race, and what is now termed "sexual preference".' Hitchens acknowledged some 'some crankish bits in the list, as when … Paul Robeson is written off as "Very anti-white".' Even so, Hitchens dismissed entirely any idea that malice played a role in the inclusion of national, sexual, and racial details and insisted that 'all too much has been made of this relatively trivial episode'. After all, 'it is true that Isaac Deutscher is listed as a "Polish Jew", and it is also true that he was a Polish Jew.' Likewise, Stephen Spender and Tom Driberg were correctly identified as homosexual. And so on. This would be more convincing were not Orwell's distaste for 'pansies' as well known to Hitchens as Orwell's recurrent suspicion of Jews ('he would vent some cliché about Jews being money-makers or literary types being queers'), and were not his racial comments so loaded with connotations of treason and antinational loyalties.[37]

It may be that all too much has been made of the list, which hardly voids the contribution Orwell made to the development of an anti-Stalinist socialism, his prescience about Zionism, and his hatred for colonialism. And Orwell, even bearing in mind his most polemical and severe statements (about pacifists, sandal wearers, muesli eaters, the left, and so on), was hardly to blame for the uses to which his work would be put by cold warriors and the CIA.

But the zeal with which Hitchens performed his white-washing duties probably arose from two sources. The first was his tendency to idealise those he admired, typically allowing only the smallest blemishes. Orwell was an ego ideal, so flaws could be admitted – but nothing too fundamental. The obverse of this, naturally, was the bitter scolding of critics who went too far. Hitchens lacerated Raymond Williams, for example, as 'the overrated doyen of cultural studies and Cambridge English, who never uttered a straightforward word' about Soviet torture, for his critical commentary on *Nineteen Eighty-four*.[38]

This was typically petulant of Hitchens. Williams was justly impugned on several accounts by Hitchens, above all for a certain amount of evasion on the question of Stalinism. But Hitchens had alighted on the least impressive or most polemical judgements made by Williams of Orwell in a series of texts. A great deal of what Williams wrote about Orwell was respectful (if grudgingly so) and discriminating. Moreover, Hitchens had been obtuse in his reading of the texts he did sample. For example, a recurring argument of Williams's was that Orwell had produced, in *Nineteen Eighty-four*, a work of incredible pessimism and despair that degraded human beings. As a work of futuristic fantasy in the guise of naturalistic realism, it extrapolated from supposed trends in the real world – towards superstatism, authoritarianism, and thought control. For Williams the whole prognosis, while obviously parodic, rested on an attitude towards power that Orwell did not possess but that his fiction did. In this context Williams took Winston's ultimate betrayal of Julia to be an affirmation at the level of fiction, that people will always betray each other – yes, it is fiction but 'it is what he makes happen'.

As Hitchens understood matters, Williams was accusing Orwell of 'recommending the course of self-abnegation and betrayal that Smith takes when he is finally broken … One reels back. Orwell *makes this happen*?' In fact, as would be clear from reading Williams, he did not accuse Orwell of desiring or recommending this end, even in his fiction. Williams knew very well what Orwell's political commitments were but perceived in his futurology (this is the future 'he made happen') the pessimistic view that people will always betray one another.[39] This is a highly debatable interpretation but, in his determination to be uncharitable, Hitchens missed the point and thus missed the opportunity for a more compelling critique. As was often the case, he proved stunningly literal, obtuse, and lacking in suppleness when dealing with someone who was too critical of one of his saints.

The second source of Hitchens's energy in rescuing Orwell on this issue is most probably his sense that, in defending 'his country', Orwell was doing something ultimately worthwhile. For Orwell's position as an intelligent, critical patriot is among his most laudable attributes, so far as Hitchens was concerned. Writing of Orwell's pieties about England, Hitchens distinguished between the latter's calm and resolute patriotism and the '"Merrie England" school', between the ambivalent, qualified defence of England and the jingoistic 'my country right or wrong'.

Orwell's writings on the English character, especially as he abandoned the revolutionary internationalism of his days in Spain with the Workers' Party of Marxist Unification (POUM) for revolutionary patriotism, could be exceptionally mawkish. He was also unapologetically sentimental about national quirks such as English cooking, tea, and the imperial measurements system. However, Hitchens asserted: 'The superficial attitude towards warm beer, brass rubbings, cathedral closes and the distant thwack of willow on leather – the whole repertoire of supposed Englishness and sentiment is a poor guide to questions of principle.'[40]

Nations are always more easily defined against (usually threatening) Others. In this light it is not surprising that Orwell's descriptions of the English character often took the form of a rudimentary comparative sociology, in which its ostensibly decent characteristics emerged as sheer contrasts with other European nations. Nor is it surprising that his patriotism was extruded in a moment of seemingly existential peril. And Orwell's sentimental evocations of old England were indissociable from his sensitivity to any conceivable threat to that England. On this Hitchens obscured far more than he clarified. For example, praising Orwell's scepticism about Unionism and rectitude on the crimes of England, Hitchens remarked that Orwell 'wrote at some length about the potential for a resurgence of Scottish nationalism, a movement which he had learned about from the elementary technique of studying, and taking seriously, the letters he received from readers'.[41]

Orwell did indeed think there was a basis for Scottish nationalism, and he had a creditable sympathy for the ways in which the Scottish working class suffered under an Anglicised ruling class. But some credit has to be subtracted for Orwell's conclusion:

At any rate, I think we should pay more attention to the small but violent separatist movements which exist within our own island. They may look very unimportant now, but, after all, the *Communist Manifesto* was once a very obscure document, and the Nazi Party only had six members when Hitler joined it.[42]

Such alarmist augury hardly attests to Orwell's good sense and perspicacity in the manner that Hitchens would suggest.

Further, the 'repertoire of Englishness' that Orwell devoted so much energy to refining, particularly during World War II, certainly had something to do with the principles he was trying to develop. In particular, having abandoned his antiwar views, which he had held roughly between 1936 and 1940, he tried to come to terms with the power that patriotism had over him – and, he thought, against all rivals, including international socialism:

> If I had to defend my reasons for supporting the war, I believe I could do so. There is no real alternative between resisting Hitler and surrendering to him … in any case I can see no argument for surrender that does not make nonsense of the Republican resistance in Spain, the Chinese resistance to Japan, etc. etc. But I don't pretend that that is the emotional basis of my actions … the long drilling patriotism which the middle classes go through had done its work, and that once England was in a serious jam it would be impossible for me to sabotage.[43]

If there was to be a socialist England, then, it would have to come to terms with this 'long drilling'. The 'suet puddings and red pillar-boxes' had entered the soul, and any prospective socialism would have to develop on the basis of intransigent national characteristics, rather than on foreign rationalisms and revolutionary theory. For Hitchens this body of writing – including not just *The Lion and the Unicorn* but also the essay 'The English People', which Orwell preferred to be suppressed – held up 'quite well' as it was 'calmly and resolutely patriotic' but not flag waving.[44]

There is something to this description, at least insofar as Orwell's stoicism and intelligence would not permit him to become an outright jingo. However, the portrait he offered of Englishness, even permitting the odd rhetorical extravagance, was culturally, if not strictly politically, conservative: the English respect for law and order, antipathy to abstraction and rationalism, preference for peaceful change, deference, xenophobia, and so on. Equally, his account of the empire, for all that it acknowledged 'its crying abuses, its stagnation in one place and exploitation in another', nonetheless verged on apologia in claiming that it 'at least has the merit of being internally peaceful' – a depiction that, if it really took no notice of the repression in India, Sudan, Iraq, and Palestine, would look absurd in contrast to the force deployed against anticolonial rebellions in the postwar period.[45]

Granted, Orwell's depiction was of an evolving, changing culture, and one in which the real popular culture was antagonistic towards the dominant culture. There was even something faintly Gramscian, to use an anachronistic term, in his approach. Nonetheless, these were the antagonisms of a family in which the wrong people were in charge, and beneath change was an irreducible core of continuity:

> What can the England of 1940 have in common with the England of 1840? But then, what have you in common with the child of five whose photograph your mother keeps on the mantelpiece? Nothing, except that you happen to be the same person.[46]

There is no inherent reason why people who live in the same nation-state, with its national language, media, and education systems, should not develop some shared characteristics. Allowing that Orwell was for the most part attempting to describe popular or working-class culture, as opposed to that which obtained for the middle or ruling class, it is on the face of it quite plausible to assay the cultural characteristics of a 'people'. And Orwell was observant, even if the trends he identified were not always borne out. The trouble is that he did not follow through with his insight into the 'long drilling' he had endured: culture must be assiduously constructed, and reconstructed, at each step in reference to new social, political, and technological forms. It cannot be assumed to be an organic entity, rather like a person.

'National culture' in its Orwellian declination was ultimately essentialist and organicist, so that he treated as essential various characteristics that are more likely to be – where not fanciful – conjunctural or historically produced. For example, it is generally the case in stable capitalist democracies that law and order commands legitimacy among most people, for most of the time. But this varies with historical experience, and antipolice subcultures have their place in Britain as elsewhere. Or again, the empiricist prejudice, which Orwell and Hitchens certainly shared, did not survive unadulterated by the expansion of higher education and the student radicalisation of the 1960s.[47] Orwell was in many senses describing aspects of the dominant ideology in Britain in his time, and by accepting these as national characteristics with deep roots in English historical experience, he tended towards a certain traditionalism that reproved much of the basis of his revolutionary politics.

Hitchens glanced lightly over these ambiguities, particularly the extent to which Orwell's early support for war was entwined with the view that Britain had to undergo a revolution to win it. Hitchens glibly referred to Orwell in this period as 'a sort of post-Trotskyist Home Guarder' but left the substance of this unexamined. The Home Guard was to be transformed into the type of organisation that could intervene in what Orwell believed was a brewing revolutionary situation and as such not only defend England but also overthrow the ruling class. This ellipsis in Hitchens's account may be because he felt that Orwell's position was tragically unrealistic and thus best not talked about. The problem is that Orwell's evolving positions were bound up with the often impressionistic sketches of the national character that Hitchens thought stood up well. A key contention of Orwell's revolutionary patriotism was that the English class system was profoundly altering, with the middle class assimilating more and more layers of the traditional working and upper classes. An intermediate stratum, often highly skilled and well educated, was rendering the old class system obsolete and becoming the basis for a revolution against a decrepit ruling class that could no longer govern. It did not turn out that the expanding layer of functionaries and technicians displaced the old class system or that it formed a basis for revolutionary or even necessarily leftist politics. The result was that Orwell was compelled to abandon his forlorn strategy for overthrowing the ruling class and gravitate towards 'democratic socialism'. Hitchens tended to treat Orwell's shifting positions as the result of his own rectitude and treated Orwell's doubts about the 'English People' essay as an example of this obsessive desire to stay on the right side of probity. Hitchens thereby minimised the extent to which Orwell passed through real, tumultuous, and often unaccounted changes in his whole worldview, representing the process as one of fine-tuning and careful adjustment. Again, Hitchens's mission was one of idealising his subject rather than revealing it.[48]

But if what Hitchens found praiseworthy in Orwell's patriotism is revealing, so is what Hitchens found blameworthy in Orwell's internationalism. For Orwell 'fell for some time into the belief that "Britain", as such or as so defined, wasn't worth fighting for'. Hitchens regarded this antiwar Orwell as merely a lapse, accounted for by frustration with 'conventional patriotism' rather than as an expression of the internationalist *trotskisant* politics he had acquired in Spain. The *real* Orwell was the patriot, revealed in 1940; the prosecutor of 'objectively pro-Fascist' pacifists; the foe of those who would betray both class and country, above all the Communists. When it came to the national question, this was the Orwell with whom Hitchens formed an imaginary identification.

In a residual cultural and emotional sense, Hitchens was a traditionalist, nostalgic for an old England of which he believed he had seen the last. Orwell's writing, and the historical experiences it expressed (middle-class upbringing, boarding school, empire, and a brush with revolutionary politics), resonated with Hitchens in many ways. But one of the ways in which it did so was in the articulation of a patriotism and cultural traditionalism that, to Hitchens, lacked the disadvantages of its noisier and more belligerent expressions. And Hitchens's patriotism would become much more bellicose, and lead him much farther to the right, than Orwell had gone.

BELATED RETORTS TO EDWARD W. SAID

Among the friendships detonated by Hitchens on his route to the right was the close, affectionate comity he had enjoyed with Edward W. Said. This is of particular interest here because of what the symbolic sacrifice of such a friendship conveyed. There is far more anguish, tenderness, and regret in Hitchens's nonetheless bitter assaults on Said than in any other polemical campaign upon which he embarked. From his first attack, in the *Atlantic* in 2003, to Said's obituary only a few months later and finally Hitchens's extended portrait of Said in *Hitch-22*, a palpable tension exists between what Hitchens feels he must write – we can take his word for it that he was motivated by conscience, as many betrayals are – and what he would write were he not sworn to play his part in this *combat à outrance* between rival civilisations.[49]

The ambivalent thrust of the assault, which simultaneously depicts Said as an exceptionally generous, urbane, sophisticated man of letters and at the same time as a vaguely duplicitous Asian possessed by an extremely one-dimensional anti-Americanism, appears to arise from the conflict between Hitchens's romanticising impulse and his demonological propensity. 'I was indistinctly aware that Edward didn't feel himself quite at liberty to say certain things,' Hitchens explains. Said exhibited mysterious inconsistencies, and, when pressed about his attitude towards a subject such as the Islamic Republic of Iran, he would make a concession about the indefensibility of the regime and then proceed as if nothing had been conceded. The key to this self-censoring, Delphic, and inconsistent Said is disclosed inter alia: 'Edward in the final instance believed that if the United States was doing something, then that thing could not by definition be a moral or ethical action.'[50] Said, then, was harbouring a profound yet extremely simple-minded anti-Americanism. This was the burden of Hitchens's final break with Said.

Hitchens resented Said's work for a number of reasons. To begin with,

Said was critical of Orwell, exhibiting a 'pronounced dislike' to which Hitchens came to feel he 'ought to have paid more attention'.[51] Salman Rushdie was another with whose distaste for Orwell Hitchens had taken issue in *Why Orwell Matters*, but he did not repudiate Rushdie's friendship and judgement in the same manner. This might suggest an element of post hoc rationalisation. Another reason was that Hitchens did not like Said's continental and theoretical analysis of literature, about which Hitchens remained defiantly sentimental. At this point John Bullshit took over.

More egregiously, though, Said was on the wrong side of the war on terror. Hitchens recalled the offences that spurred him to take action:

> In the special edition of the London Review of Books published to mark the events of September 11, 2001, Edward painted a picture of an almost fascist America where Arab and Muslim citizens were being daily terrorized by pogroms, these being instigated by men like Paul Wolfowitz who had talked of 'ending' the regimes that sheltered Al Quaeda.

Just as treacherously, Said had written of the wave of looting that swept Baghdad after the fall of the Ba'ath regime as, Hitchens claimed, 'a deliberate piece of United States vandalism, perpetrated in order to shear the Iraqi people of their cultural patrimony and demonstrate to them their new servitude'.[52] Given the grief that these accusations gave their author, it seems almost pedantic to say that neither can be verified by reference to the sources.

Thus outraged, Hitchens began to brood on the ways in which his personal and political disagreements with Said were culminating, until Hitchens was presented with the opportunity to review an anniversary edition of Said's *Orientalism*. Felicitously, Hitchens's conscience vindicated his action in advance: 'When the *Atlantic* invited me to review Edward's revised edition, I decided I'd suspect myself more if I declined than if I agreed.'[53] If conscience does not necessarily make cowards of us all, it can nonetheless let us down terribly. In this case it goaded Hitchens into laying bare what must have been obvious to his friends and comrades, but which they had tolerantly overlooked: his utter philistinism. This, for example, is how he explained *Orientalism*: 'Said characterized Western scholarship about the East as a conscious handmaiden of power and subordination. Explorers, missionaries, archaeologists, linguists – all had been part of a colonial enterprise.'[54]

In essence, Hitchens asserted, Said's case was that the Orientalists were producing misleading and unfair representations of the East. And he proceeded with this reproach:

> It is also true that Arab, Indian, Malay, and Iranian societies can operate on a false if not indeed deluded view of 'the West' … there exists a danger in too strong a counterposition between 'East' and 'West'. The 'West' has its intellectual and social troughs, just as the 'East' has its pinnacles … Cultural-political interaction, then, must be construed as dialectical. Edward Said was in a prime position to be a 'negotiator' here. In retrospect, however, it can be argued that he chose a one-sided approach and employed rather a broad brush … [according to Orientalism] every instance of European curiosity about the East, from Flaubert to Marx, was part of a grand design to exploit and remake what Westerners saw as a passive, rich, but ultimately contemptible 'Oriental' sphere.[55]

One might conclude that this caricature – for caricature it is – was malicious, were there not grounds to suspect that its author believed it to be, loaded sarcasm aside, an absolutely authentic depiction. (As if to underline this, much of the article is actually plagiarised from the book it is allegedly reviewing.)[56] The ways in which Hitchens travestied Said are worth stating briefly, if only to get a measure of his befuddlement.

Orientalism by no means posits the conspiracy theory, at once vastly intricate and unidimensional, that Hitchens described. Orientalism is a discourse, in the sense developed by Michel Foucault – a form of power-knowledge that constructs its object for investigation and determines the ways in which the object, in this case the 'Orient', can be meaningfully talked about. The scope of this discourse, manifest in the works of archaeologists, philologists, historians, and writers, beginning with Napoleon's invasion of Egypt in 1798, expanded through the high tide of nineteenth-century imperialism but less by dint of a 'grand design' than by the logic of colonial possession. Dominating the Middle East and southern Asia afforded a certain type of knowledge.

As follows from the foregoing, Said's point was not that there is a 'real' Orient lurking behind a set of misrepresentations. Rather, the Orient itself was a construction of a type of knowing bound up with power; it existed only insofar as it was known. This is one reason why the critique of *Orientalism*, espoused by Hitchens and others, that complains of Said's obliviousness to Eastern misapprehensions of the West, what has been called 'Occidentalism', misses its mark. Put briefly, there is no history of colonial or imperial control of Europe or North America by

India, Egypt, or Japan, through which 'the West' could be constructed. Insofar as 'the West' is an object of knowledge, investigation, and speculation, this has been overwhelmingly a concern of European and American writers and academics.[57] Another reason is that Said was in fact known to criticise certain representations of 'the West' that went on in Arab-language media. His regular columns in *Al-Ahram* were notable for just this trait.[58] Hitchens actually acknowledged this, only to deflect the issue onto another complaint: 'He is a source of stern admonition to the uncritical, insulated Arab elites and intelligentsia. But for some reason … he cannot allow that direct Western engagement in the region is legitimate.'[59] How an earlier, more Orwellian, Hitchens might have reacted to using a euphemism like 'engagement' to describe, say, the Soviet invasion of Hungary, one can only guess.

In fairness, then, Hitchens's incomprehension was probably not solely the product of his being, as Terry Eagleton put it, 'uneasy with abstract ideas' and 'stridently simplistic whenever he strays into the realms of science, philosophy, or theology'. At least part of it owed to Hitchens's belief in and commitment to the concept of the Orient as the object of 'Western engagement', that is, to the East–West binary that underpins Orientalism. From a perspective in which the Orient really exists independent of any relationship to colonialism, about which it is possible to have true or false impressions, it would indeed seem that *Orientalism* simply debunks unfair stereotypes – and at that in a grossly broad-brush fashion.

Perhaps the most enlightening passages in Hitchens's reproach – with regard to the author rather than the subject – are those contrasting Said with Karl Marx on India. On this subject one would expect Hitchens's critique to come from the left. But in fact, consistent with the whole appraisal, Marx is conscripted to an argument from the right. In a reasonably well-known Marxist critique of Said, the Indian literary critic Aijaz Ahmad briskly takes issue with the whole theoretical edifice of *Orientalism*, far more vehemently than Hitchens himself (albeit not as gustily as Ibn Warraq's *Defending the West*, which Hitchens characterised as 'the best critique' of *Orientalism*).[60] Ahmad reserved particular scorn for the representation of Marx's writing on India that, Said averred, abjured the humanity of colonial subjects. For Said it appeared that Marx treated Indians as a raw material for his heroic vision of progress, which the British Empire was imposing on the subcontinent in its savage way. Ahmad disputed this reading quite forcefully, citing the scripture, as it were, to show that Marx by no means dehumanised Indians in this way or subscribed to a simple view of imperialist progress.[61] Hitchens's approach was quite different, in that he thought that Said was correct about the elements of Marx's approach to colonialism and merely wrong in his valuation of them.

According to Hitchens, Marx

> thought that the British had brought modernity to India in the form of printing presses, railways, the telegraph, and steamship contact with other cultures. Marx didn't believe that they had done this out of the kindness of their hearts. 'England, it is true, in causing a social revolution in Hindustan was actuated only by the vilest interests,' he wrote, '… but that is not the question. The question is, can mankind fulfill its destiny without a fundamental revolution in the social state of Asia?' … Said spent a lot of time 'puzzling' (his word) over Marx's ironies here: how could a man of professed human feeling justify conquest and exploitation? The evident answer – that conquest furnished an alternative to the terrifying serfdom and stagnation of antiquity, and that creation can take a destructive form – need have nothing to do with what Said calls 'the old inequality between East and West'.[62]

It is not that Marx's writing on colonialism wholly lacks this attention to creative destruction. But Hitchens's interpretation of Marx relied entirely on his earliest writings on this subject, which rested too heavily on a false impression of the real state of Indian social relations and were in error about the impact of the British Empire on India. Nor was this a novel interpretation of Marx from Hitchens's perspective. He had, in his defence of Paul Scott's *The Raj Quartet* in 1985, quoted from the same early material, noting that Marx had considered the British 'superior to Hindu civilization' but suggesting that, in time, the British would lay the basis for India to have outgrown (Hitchens's word) colonial rule. Marx's arguments on India evolved, partly in light of accumulating evidence that British capitalist development had been 'useless for the Hindoos' and that they had been subject to a 'bleeding process with a vengeance'. More to the point, he and Engels developed a wider repertoire of writing on empire that cumulatively repudiated the view that capitalist imperialism was a progressive development, culminating in Marx's writing on Ireland, which formed the basis for socialist anti-imperialism in the twentieth century.[63] So, in rebutting Said, Hitchens actually repudiated an important aspect of the Marxism he had positioned himself to defend.

Shortly after Hitchens's attack on Said, he was forwarded an article in which 'Edward quoted some sentences about the Iraq war that he off-handedly described as "racist". The sentences in question had been written by me. I felt myself assailed by a reaction that was at once hot-eyed and frigidly cold.'[64] After this he never spoke to Said again and did not attend his funeral. This was a heart-breaking conclusion to such a friendship. But also peculiar, for Hitchens would have known that Said considered some of his views racist. Asked to comment on Hitchens's exuberant support for cluster bombing, Said had told the *Nation* in 2002: 'He's gone back to nineteenth-century gunboat diplomacy – go hit the wogs.' At the same time Hitchens did not risk giving his readers the opportunity to agree with Said by republishing the sentences, or naming the journal or article in which they had been quoted, never mind written, or the date of publication.[65]

In all likelihood Hitchens knew of the effect that his attack would have but sacrificed the friendship nonetheless. 'If Hitchens were here', D. D. Guttenplan suggests,

> he would say that 'each man kills the thing he loves.' And I think that Edward represented for him the deepest, truest form of the radical engagement that had the most powerful hold on him. So, if he was really going to move to the right, he had to get rid of Edward.

Tariq Ali takes a similar view: Hitchens's deathbed assault on Said was a signal that Hitchens would never again write the things he once had about Palestine. And indeed he never again did. Guttenplan wrote to him during the Israeli invasion of Lebanon in 2006 to inquire about his extraordinary muteness on the subject. Guttenplan recalled that in 1982 he had met Hitchens at the height of Israel's previous invasion of Lebanon, just at the end of the Nuclear FREEZE protest, and that Hitchens had been furious about the peace movement's refusal to mobilise against the Israeli invasion. It was the most important thing in the world in 1982 yet not enough to merit more than one equivocal article in 2006.[66]

The attack on Said thus confirmed the triumph of those aspects of Hitchens's political personality that had always been indulgent towards aspects of colonialism, Eurocentric, and inclined to a vulgar view of historical progress in which subjugated peoples needed British tutelage. Now it seemed that American tutoring was needed, to turn back a recrudescence of barbarism in the 'East', and Hitchens had provided himself with the rationale for the necessary adjustments on his part.

3 GUILTY AS SIN: THEOPHOBIA, FROM RUSHDIE TO THE WAR ON TERROR

I have one consistency, which is [being] against the totalitarian – on the left and on the right. The totalitarian, to me, is the enemy – the one that's absolute, the one that wants control over the inside of your head, not just your actions and your taxes. And the origins of that are theocratic, obviously.

– Christopher Hitchens, 'Richard Dawkins
Interviews Christopher Hitchens'

The idea that if once we got rid of religion, all problems of this kind would vanish, seems wild. Whatever may have been its plausibility in the eighteenth century, when it first took the centre of the stage, it is surely just a distraction today. It is, however, one often used by those who do not want to think seriously on this subject.

– Mary Midgley, *Wickedness*

LITTLE HITCHENS, BIG GOD

There usually comes a time when a child begins to notice the inconsistencies and absurdities in the silly stories that grown-ups tell them in order to get them to behave. Christopher Hitchens was nine – a little late, if I may say so. His teacher one day exclaimed how wonderful it was that God had made the trees and grass green so that they would be pleasant to the eye, and he simply knew that the teacher had it wrong: 'The eyes were adjusted to nature, and not the other way about.'[1] After this he began 'to notice other oddities' such as, if Jesus could heal a blind person, why not heal blindness? Why were prayers not answered? Why was sex so toxic a subject?

Such 'faltering and childish objections', as Hitchens called them, are not disgraceful in a child.[2] Yet what is surprising is how frequently demotic reasoning of this type returns in Hitchens's writing on religion. It may be objected that this is because, in his words, 'no religion can meet them with any satisfactory answer.' But this is far from true, as I will demonstrate. At any rate, it is hardly a good reason to persist with such humdrum observations. Just as curious is the literal-minded John Bullishness with which the author approached his subject and above all his careless errors and ham-fisted generalisations. By Hitchens's own standards, this combination – obviousness, literalism, and bullshit – constitutes a triple-crown howler. To this extent the author was a poor atheist. He made secularism seem uninteresting and materialism incondite. Worse, at key moments chauvinism, paranoid alarums for civilisational warfare, and downright racism took hold of his onslaught against religion.

While Hitchens's fundamental view of religion throughout his political life did not alter substantially, the dramatic alteration of the role of antitheism as an element in his politics and idiolect really began in and around 2005, and the motivation for this was partially opportunistic. By this I do not simply mean that Hitchens viewed the success of books by Sam Harris, Daniel Dennett, and Richard Dawkins and spotted the opportunity of a lifetime. As ever with Hitchens, we can hardly discount this as a motive, and the decision to follow the others into that market did in fact do more than anything else to establish his reputation. In short, it displaced his recent focus on prosecuting the ideological war on behalf of the occupation of Iraq, which was then falling into disrepute amid escalating bloodshed and the revelation of torture. In fact, his writing about religion sufficed both as displacement and as explanation, since it purported to show that the overthrow of Saddam Hussein would have been the liberation he promised had it not been for religion's poisoning everything. To this extent *God Is Not Great* works as an entertaining expiation of the sins of imperialism and indeed of capitalism.

The function of this antitheism was structurally analogous to what Irving Howe characterised as Stalinophobia. This referred to a particular mutation of Cold War politics in which former elements of the anti-Stalinist left allowed their hatred for the Soviet Union to assume a grossly disproportionate role in their politics. The Bogey-Scapegoat of Stalinism justified a new alliance with the right, obliviousness towards the permanent injustices of capitalist society, and a tolerance for repressive practices conducted in the name of the 'Free World'. In a roughly isomorphic fashion Hitchens's preoccupation with religion, and particularly religious politics, authorised not just a 'blind eye' to the injustices of capitalism and empire but a vigorous advocacy of the same. Worse, he shared with many of the 'new atheists' the dogma that, in terms of egregiousness, all religions are equal, and Islam is more equal than others. And this segued into a virulently reactionary position that ended up corroborating the hard right.

PRELUDE: THE RUSHDIE AFFAIR

The persecution of Salman Rushdie by the clerical authorities of the Islamic Republic of Iran was only the culmination of a reaction to the publication of *The Satanic Verses* that began among some Muslims in the United Kingdom and rapidly spread to India, Bangladesh, Sri Lanka, Indonesia, Singapore, apartheid South Africa, and Venezuela, all states that banned the novel no more than a year after its publication. In the United Kingdom itself a number of bookstores were attacked, and a campaign was mounted to get the book withdrawn from circulation. Several months after the reaction began, Ayatollah Khomeini 'condemned to death' the author, publishers, and editors of *The Satanic Verses*. The author was compelled to go into hiding. In this context Rushdie relied on a coalition of intellectuals and writers – by no means a small set – to mount his defence. Most vocal among these was Christopher Hitchens.

Hitchens had first met Salman Rushdie at a friend's Notting Hill pad in the mid-1980s. The writer was a left-winger whose books had satirised the politics of the Indian subcontinent, and US imperialism in Nicaragua. As was often the case with Hitchens, he tended to idealise Rushdie. In *Hitch-22* and elsewhere the figure of Rushdie that emerges is ironic, hyperliterate, and impossibly witty. 'There seemed', Hitchens wrote, 'to be no book or poem in English that he hadn't read, and his first language had been Urdu.'[3] Yet, Hitchens added, 'I like to think that my reaction would have been the same if I hadn't known Salman at all.'[4] We can take it for granted that Hitchens meant this. But it also seems reasonable to suppose that his impatience with Rushdie's critics, not all of whom deserved the rancour he directed at them, owed something to this friendship.

Hitchens engaged in this debate as a defender of liberal humanism (the idiom of Rushdie's novels) and free speech, and as an opponent of the ethnic absolutism implied in the patronising response of those who assumed that Muslims *in toto* were offended by Rushdie's text. The 'condescending Western Islamologists', Hitchens said, 'granted Khomeini his first premiss by assuming that there is something called "Islam" or "the Muslim world": something undifferentiated and amorphous that can, like an individual, be "offended". [5]

Hitchens also punctured the manifest resentment towards Rushdie, a man whose literary gifts undoubtedly aroused a conventional racist image of wily Orientals excessively endowed with intelligence and all too susceptible to decadent intellectualism. [6]

Yet the discussion does not end there. On two related issues, Hitchens either lacked insight or was obstinately purblind: the offence that might legitimately be taken from the book, and the ensuing politics of condemnation – not only of Rushdie but of Rushdie's detractors. If anything, Hitchens insisted that these issues were beside the point. And, if the sole issue at stake was whether Salman Rushdie should be allowed to be murdered for a bounty, or have his books suppressed, then they would be. But the 'Rushdie affair' included a great deal more than this. Hitchens complained:

> The centers of several British cities were choked by hysterical crowds, all demanding not just less freedom for the collective … but also screaming for a deeply reactionary attack on the rights of the individual – the destruction of an author's work and even the taking of an author's life. That this ultrareactionary mobocracy was composed mainly of people with brown skins ought to have made no difference. [7]

Yet, if one was to understand how Rushdie's work had come to be implicated in struggles over the position of Muslims in European and North American societies, it *did* have to make a difference. No offence arising from the publication of *The Satanic Verses*, a complex work of art, could merit the death penalty. However, it makes no sense to rule out further discussion, as if to consider the possibility of being legitimately offended was to mandate acts of tomecide in Grosvenor Square. And this is exactly what Hitchens had a tendency to do.

To begin with, as ever when dealing with his idols, Hitchens minimised any potential problem from every angle. As a result, while he was by no means prepared to concede that blasphemy deserved to be punished, much less by death, he went much further, insisting that no one could possibly take legitimate offence at *The Satanic Verses*. And he acknowledged only one possible cause of religious offence, an unflattering representation of Muhammad in the book, in words 'spoken by a sick man, suffering from paranoid schizophrenia, in a dream, in which he believes himself to be the Archangel Gabriel.' [8] This was disingenuous.

Even if not *in persona propria*, the novel is studded with hardly flattering satirical references to the Prophet, Mecca, the Prophet's wives, and historical Muslim figures such as Saladin.

Undoubtedly, Hitchens had his answer to such complaints ready: if you are offended, so much the worse for you. But this is one of the ways in which he had a tendency to substitute affect – in this case the sentiment of belligerent defiance – for analysis. The question, once rousing sentiment has passed, remains: how was it possible that the novel, a mordant satirical fantasy exploring the usual themes of cultural hybridity and plurality, which Rushdie expected to offend only some of the more conservative clerisy, aroused Muslim antipathy from London to Lahore and resulted in widespread bans? Clearly, much of this took place without reference to the novel's real satirical intent, whereas the controversy acted on political and historical factors that neither the novelist nor his detractors had created.

Absent a careful reading of the politics of this, the tendency is for the explanation to lapse into cultural essentialism, or 'Londonistan'-style eristic. Hitchens at one stage paid lip service to the issue of imperialism but was too quick to extricate this from the issue at hand:

> I have written (as has Salman Rushdie on several occasions) about the injustices done to Moslem peoples by Western imperialism. Come to think of it, Rushdie has been rather more forthright on this than either *The Atlantic* or *The Washington Monthly*. But that's not the point here. The issue is the right of Rushdie to make literary use of holy writ and the right of others, including Moslems, to be an audience for such writing.[9]

The injustices referred to here are not beside the point, but they are not the whole point. The relationship of 'Western imperialism' to various 'Moslem peoples', including to those Muslims living in imperialist societies, was obviously a critical issue on which the whole Rushdie affair pivoted. But by skating over this so lightly, Hitchens missed the opportunity to capture the way in which that relationship had altered. There had been many realignments of forces in which Muslims resisted imperialism, from Bandung to the Tricontinental Conference or from Indonesian communism to Syrian nationalism. But most of these forces were defeated or had degenerated. Sometime between the 1967 war and the Iranian Revolution, the ascendant form of resistant politics had become one or other variant of Islamism. And, as Hitchens's friend Edward Said pointed out in *Covering Islam*, this was coterminous with a reconfiguration of imperialism itself, as it identified its subject and target increasingly as Islam.[10] With the dominant forces in the US increasingly including an alliance between religious fundamentalists and hard-line Zionists, the terrain was favourable for stark contrasts and ethnic absolutisms.

In the context of the Rushdie affair, such ethnic absolutism was only redoubled and reinforced, as Muslims living in the imperialist socie-ties found themselves increasingly pigeonholed into identitarian boxes and as their religious identity was itself racialised.[11] All this inescap-ably shaped the reactions not just to Rushdie's novel but to the whole sequence of events, protests, murders, recriminations, bannings, arti-cles, and documentaries that followed from it. For most participants the entire saga was saturated with these meanings and could not be limited to the issue of free speech that Hitchens preferred to fight. As a result he either ignored or glossed over these details and thus in fact missed out on most of the argument.

For this reason, among others, Hitchens's typically mean-spirited attacks on those like Michael Dummett, whose position was more equivocal than he liked, simply fell flat. Hitchens's memoir, recounting the contretemps, hysterically characterised Dummett and John Berger as members of the 'multi-culti', postmodern left 'somehow in league with political Islam' for criticising Rushdie and expressing worries about the rise of anti-Muslim racism.[12] Dummett and Berger's posi-tions had some real weaknesses, but Hitchens was hardly the person to anatomise them. In the same memoir, moreover, it becomes clear that Hitchens had been totally nonplussed by Said's argument in *Covering Islam* and suspected some form of covert apologia for the Islamic Republic was lurking behind the sophisticated apparatus of politicised cultural criticism. Hitchens's neglect of the wider politics of the situa-tion, combined with a certain metropolitan disdain for the religious, slipped into a strident, huffy approach that anathematised his oppo-nents in a way that anticipated somewhat the invective of the war on terror.

There is also Hitchens's emerging attitude towards Islam itself to register. For a host of Islamophobic commentators, the Rushdie affair signified a civilisational clash between the West and Islam. Daniel Pipes, for example, was contemptuous of any possibility of Rushdie's finding peace in any concord between these ostensible rivals. Hitchens was, for quite a long time, bilious about such portents. No suicide bombings had occurred in the name of the ayatollah's fatwa. The editorials and clerical bluster in Iran had yielded little.[13] Any idea of a civilisational battle, a 'fight to the finish' with Islam, was mocked.

Yet it would be misleading to leave it at that. Hitchens's writing about Islam in this period, though rebuffing a certain facile absolutism to which he was later susceptible, was far from unproblematic. At times his attitudes in *this* affair foreshadowed his later Islamophobia. Furthermore, the urge to expunge any rational kernel from what he called 'Islamic fury' led him to query whether 'the damn thing didn't possess a hideously energetic life of its own', independent of 'material conditions'.[14] This, as I will show, reflects a long-standing concern of Hitchens's. Though he presented his critique of religion as a Marxist one, his habit of either ignoring or travestying Marx's arguments about religion demonstrate that Hitchens profoundly disagreed with them, precisely because of Marx's tendency to look for what is rational in religious behaviour.

A final chapter in this sad tale came when the British state decided to offer Rushdie an Order of the British Empire in 2007. By this time Hitchens had cut off his former allies on the left and thoroughly reinvented himself a die-hard opponent of all-religion-but-especially-Islam. Inevitably, the patronising debate arose as to whether Rushdie should have been nominated for such an honour. Had this man not deeply offended Muslims? Was this not a further insult and (implicitly) an unnecessary risk to take on behalf of a foreigner? Hitchens had an opportunity to intervene pointedly in this facile controversy. He rehearsed the arguments he had made at the time of Khomeini's fatwa, denying that Muslims could – all billion of them – be identified with those who had threatened Rushdie with death and noting the calumny on Muslims that this represented. He defended Rushdie's literary achievements and above all the right of the British state to issue awards as it saw fit, not to be pushed around by … Pakistan. This was a spirited performance that contrasted with the slimy argument made by Shirley Williams that such an award was perhaps unwise as it would inflame Muslim opinion.

But the claim that such an award is unsuitable for someone who has offended so many Muslims might have had a point if only the follow-up had been that to truly merit recognition from the British Empire, merely offending Muslims through a work of fiction is just not enough. It simply did not seem to occur to Hitchens to say that such an award was an inherently absurd thing or that accepting it constituted genuflection to an absurd institution.

JOHN BULL READS THE BIBLE

> *The bulls Hitchens chose were old and lumbering ... so he was never in any danger. Kissinger, long out of power; the wounded Clinton; the pathetically, not-so-sainted Mother Teresa. And of course the most pathetic, lumbering bull of all, God.*
>
> – Lesley Hazleton, comparing Hitchens to a bullfighter

God Is Not Great scrutinises the texts of ancient and modern religions with the eye of a red-faced accountant perturbed by some piece of fanciful bookkeeping. The result is an indictment charging religion with

- Presenting a false picture of the world to the innocent and the credulous
- The doctrine of blood sacrifice
- The doctrine of atonement
- The doctrine of eternal reward and/or punishment
- The imposition of impossible tasks and rules.[15]

These asseverations were argued in turn in a terse series of passages in which Hitchens attacked 'a straw God', an 'absurdly literal, anthropomorphised, fundamentalist idea of God', or indeed an 'idolatrous notion of God'.[16] Hitchens had already justified a literal reading of religious texts on the ground that 'the apologetic "modern Christian" who argues faintly that of course the Bible isn't meant to be taken literally is saying that it isn't the word of God. He is, thereby, revising his faith out of existence.' Thus the whole corpus of religious texts must be read either exclusively in the literal mode or not read at all.[17] But why should 'the word of God' be literal? This could be answered only in reference to theological traditions of interpretation, about which Hitchens displayed remarkable ignorance.

Indeed, moments in Hitchens's writing give the impression that what he most resented about religion was its ability to override the utilitarian calculations that keep everyday life more or less predictable. All very well when ventilating about the supererogatory nature of some religious prohibition, but when he complained of the parable of the lilies that it encouraged disregard of 'thrift, innovation, family life and so forth', he indeed cut the figure of an 'indignant bank manager'.[18]

Many of Hitchens's errors were mundane. He thus generously endowed a key source of his, Fawn Brodie, with a doctorate and falsely attributed the coinage *totalitarianism* to Victor Serge.[19] Compounding simple errors of fact, though, was a litany of theological pratfalls. Terry Eagleton points out a number of these:

> Hitchens's *God Is Not Great* is littered with elementary theological howlers. We learn that the God of the Old Testament never speaks of solidarity and compassion; that Christ has no human nature; and that the doctrine of resurrection means that he did not die.[20]

Further theological errors include the claim that 'the Jews borrow shamelessly from Christians in the pathetic hope of a celebration [Hanukkah] that coincides with "Christmas" ', whereas the origin of Hanukkah predates Christianity, and thus Christmas, and is supposed to have been celebrated by Jesus himself. Likewise, Hitchens averred that in order to be redeemed by Christ,

> I have to accept that I am responsible for the flogging and mocking and crucifixion, in which I had no say and no part, and agree that every time I decline this responsibility, or that I sin in word or deed, I am intensifying the agony of it. Furthermore, I am required to believe that the agony was necessary in order to compensate for an earlier crime in which I also had no part, the sin of Adam … Thus my own guilt in the matter is deemed 'original' and inescapable.[21]

On the contrary, as C. B. Moss noted, 'Strictly speaking, original sin is not sin at all, but a weakness leading to sin, just as a weak chest is not consumption.' Or, as Eagleton wrote, the

> prevalence of greed, idolatry, and delusion, the depth of our instinct to dominate and possess, the dull persistence of injustice and exploitation, the chronic anxiety which leads us to hate, maim and exploit, along with the sickness, suffering and despair which Jesus associates with evil. All this is what Christianity knows as original sin.[22]

God Is Not Great demands – as do most of the works of the 'new atheists' – that the Abrahamic religions explain the incompatibility of the Creation story with the findings of contemporary natural and physical sciences. Hitchens asserts: 'The creation myths of all peoples have long been known to be false, and have fairly recently been replaced by infinitely superior and more magnificent explanations.'[23]

This strident view relies upon an unproblematised 'scientific realism' – in brief, the view that the world described by science is the real world, which exists independently of theorising about it. This is by no means obviously the case. The majority of scientific theories have been erroneous. A religious narrative that conflicted with the concept of the phlogiston or the ether would by no means be considered falsified by these concepts today. The record of failure permits a pessimistic meta-induction from past experience, to wit, that scientific theories must in general fail to describe the world as it really is. Even supposing a weaker version of this meta-induction – that there is no necessary progress towards greater knowledge of the world in science – and a high probability of ongoing error, there is every possibility that the scientific theories being invoked to invalidate religious narratives are themselves false. The point here is not to relativise scientific knowledge in order to cut it down to size but rather to underline that it is constantly mutating. Even if one were to convincingly rebut a theological claim in light of today's science, this would be no surety against finding one's argument in tatters tomorrow.

This scientistic approach has another problem. As Terry Eagleton points out, it is mistaken to treat religious narratives as rivalling science for explanations of the physical world. One may as well query the relevance of the *Rubaiyat* of Omar Khayyam in the explanation of natural phenomena. Only by taking a severely reductive and literal approach to the Abrahamic texts, which would be a heterodox view among the religious, can one in all seriousness counterpose the Creation myth to quantum mechanics and find the former at fault for its incompatibility. Finally, even if one accepts the literal reading of the Creation myth, the proper context for evaluating its worth as science is the state of knowledge prevailing at the time of its writing, the Iron Age. In this sense the Genesis story's description of the planets and other heavenly bodies, as not personal gods but objects susceptible to physical laws, was a revolutionary idea in its time.

A further example of literal-minded obtuseness is Hitchens's reading of Abraham's near sacrifice of his son Isaac. Here, Hitchens thundered, there is no 'softening the plain meaning of this frightful story', which is the Almighty's sanction of child murder. The literalism is compounded by the absence of contextual awareness. The ancient Israelite readers of this story, as well as their neighbours in pagan societies, would have been accustomed to the idea of human sacrifice. In its context the function of the story was thus precisely to outlaw the killing of humans.[24]

Similarly, Hitchens complained that religions have historically 'staunchly resisted' the translation of their texts – the Talmud, the Bible, the Quran – into the language of the common people. He remonstrated that this demonstrates a desire on the part of the arbiters of faith to keep the people in ignorance. Again, even with a will to believe the worst about religion, this claim is impossible to sustain. William Hamblin of Brigham Young University points out:

> In reality, the translation of religious texts has been a major cultural phenomenon in ancient and medieval times and has steadily increased through the present. The Bible, of course, is the most translated book in the history of the world. According to the United Bible Societies, it has been translated into 2,167 languages, with another 320 in process. And this is by no means merely a modern phenomenon. The Bible was also the most widely translated book in the ancient world … The translation history of Buddhist scriptures is precisely the same – and again, precisely the opposite of Hitchens's claim … The earliest translations of the Qur'an appeared within a couple of centuries of Muhammad's death. By the tenth century there were extensive commentaries (tafsir) on the Qur'an in Arabic, Persian, and Turkish – the three great cultural languages of medieval Islamic civilization. These included a word-for-word grammatical analysis of the Arabic text, thereby providing translations. In the Middle Ages there were also numerous interlinear translations of the Qur'an. In addition, the Qur'an was translated by non-Muslims, largely for polemical purposes. It appeared in Greek in the ninth century, Syriac before the eleventh, and Latin in the twelfth …
>
> Hitchens laments that 'devout men like Wycliffe, Coverdale, and Tyndale were burned alive for even attempting early translations' (p. 125) of the Bible into vernacular literature … Far from being burned at the stake, John Wycliffe (1330–1384) died of natural causes while hearing Catholic mass in his parish church. Miles Coverdale likewise died unburned in 1568 at the age of eighty-one. Of the three translators mentioned by Hitchens, only William Tyndale … was burned at the stake. But Tyndale's execution in 1536 was as much for his opposition to Henry VIII's divorce – entailing what was viewed as a treasonous rejection of the Succession Act – as it was for his translation efforts.[25]

The pivot of this argument, however, is the supposed centrality of vernacular interpretation of religious texts to the possibility of a reformation. Thus the Gutenberg press made possible the Lutheran movement,

Müntzerism, Calvinism, Anglicanism, Methodism, and innumerable schisms and splits subsequent to the translation of the Bible from Latin. And so *God Is Not Great* laments the absence of a reformation of Islam – indeed, what Hitchens imagines is the impossibility of such change. I will return to this, but first it is necessary to underline just how substantial is the freight borne by this claim.

SOFT ON RELIGION, SOFT ON THE CAUSES OF RELIGION: GOD'S SURPRISING OMNIPOTENCE

> *God saved Christopher Hitchens from the right. Nobody who detested God as viscerally, intelligently, originally, and comically as he did could stay in the pocket of god-bothered American conservatism for long.*
>
> – Salman Rushdie, 'Christopher Hitchens, 1949–2011'

> *Thank you for sharing your battle with cancer in that remarkable interview. There's no telling how many folks you will inspire, whether you think it works or not. I truly will pray for you. Fight on. You contribute meaningfully to our country's discourse. God bless.*
>
> – George W. Bush, letter to Christopher Hitchens

'Name me an ethical statement made or an action performed by a believer that could not have been made or performed by a non-believer.'[26] Thus did Christopher Hitchens rebuff the claims of religion to provide a basis for moral conduct. But the converse could just as well be put to him: is it possible to name an ethically repugnant statement or action made or performed by a believer that could not have been made or performed by a nonbeliever? Child abuse, misogyny, genocide, rape, chauvinism, falsehood, enslavement, oppression – for what rebarbative action or creed does religion itself bear singular and exclusive responsibility?

Reading *God Is Not Great*, one is surprised how frequently Hitchens undermines his own thesis: the immovable faith that he displays in the real earthly power of God. The book makes two essential points – that God is not great and that religion poisons everything – and constantly refutes the first point in supporting the second. In this sense Hitchens was a true believer. He was inclined to maintain that the worst political outcomes were almost single-handedly produced by religion. Everything from the occupation of Iraq to the troubles in Northern Ireland to the Israel–Palestine conflict would have been resolved much sooner were it not for the religious factor. On Iraq he explained:

When the Coalition forces crossed the Iraqi border, they found Saddam's army dissolving like a sugar lump in hot tea, but met with some quite tenacious resistance from a paramilitary group, stiffened with foreign jihadists, called the Fedayeen Saddam. One of the jobs of this group was to execute anybody who publicly welcomed the Western intervention, and some revolting public hangings and mutilations were soon captured on video for all to see … Not one single minute of breathing space was allowed. Everybody knows the sequel. The supporters of al-Qaeda, led by a Jordanian jailbird named Abu Musab al-Zarqawi, launched a frenzied campaign of murder and sabotage … Before long, Shia death squads, often garbed in police uniforms, were killing and torturing random members of the Sunni Arab faith. The surreptitious influence of the neighbouring 'Islamic Republic' of Iran was not difficult to detect, and in some Shia areas also it became dangerous to be an unveiled woman or a secular person … Religion poisons everything.

On Israel–Palestine:

Two peoples of roughly equivalent size had a claim to the same land. The solution was, obviously, to create two states side by side. Surely something so self-evident was within the wit of man to encompass? And so it would have been, decades ago, if the messianic rabbis and mullahs and priests could have been kept out of it … Religion poisons everything.

And Northern Ireland:

In Belfast, I have seen whole streets burned out by sectarian warfare between different sects of Christianity, and interviewed people whose relatives and friends have been kidnapped and killed or tortured by rival religious death squads … (Even the word 'drill' makes me queasy: a power tool of that kind was often used to destroy the kneecaps of those who fell foul of the religious gangs.)[27]

Elsewhere, he argued that 'if you're writing about the history of the 1930s and the rise of totalitarianism, you can take out the word "fascist", if you want, for Italy, Portugal, Spain, Czechoslovakia and Austria and replace it with "extreme-right Catholic party".'[28]

There is a none-too-subtle lacuna in each of these examples. For instance, in discussing the 'religious gangs' of Northern Ireland, which are nothing of the kind, Hitchens did not deign to discuss the source of the conflict, which was the annexation of the North of Ireland by the British Empire. Without this there would have been no need to create a sectarian 'Orange' statelet in the North. Similarly, in discussing the civil war in Lebanon, he raised Hezbollah's use of suicide bombing without mentioning the US Marines against whom they were deployed.[29] On Israel–Palestine it fell to Anthony Blair in a debate with Hitchens to point out that the reasons for the enduring conflict also had something to do with the political actors involved.[30] Naturally, Blair did not alight upon what Hitchens once knew but had somehow forgotten: that the major obstacle to a peaceful settlement is the Israeli state itself and the politics of expansionist ethnic nationalism upon which it is founded.

Iraq is, for many obvious reasons, the major blind spot here. If Hitchens had turned a blind eye to the religious soldiers fighting alongside him in Bosnia, he actively ignored as far as possible the alliance between the Parties of God and the imperialist armies in the governing of Iraq. Specifically, he did not hazard to notice that the Supreme Iraqi Islamic Council, a formerly Tehran-based organisation with a Khomeinist perspective, had been used to govern the South, had supplied the personnel for the 'Iraqification' of the post-Ba'athist state, and had been incorporated fully into the apparatuses of repression created, funded, and trained by the occupation forces under General David Petraeus, whom Hitchens idolised. (The most notorious of these apparatuses, the grisly Wolves Brigade belonging to the Special Police Commandos, participated in the ethnic cleansing during Iraq's collapse into bloody civil war.) Likewise, Hitchens's representation of the Iraqi insurgency as purely a religious reflux, with at most a Ba'athist auxiliary, is simply incompatible with all available evidence, including intelligence reports in the US itself.[31]

This is not to say that Hitchens does not draw attention to, and justifiably damn, concrete abuses and crimes perpetrated by the religious precisely on the basis of their religious beliefs. But he is not always the best person to make this case. Among Hitchens's criticisms of religion was what he considered was its opposition to the liberation of women, and their reproductive rights. Yet, if the notion of Hitchens as a feminist is unconvincing, it is not only because of his trivial shock-jock commentary on why women are not funny (unless they are 'hefty or dykey or Jewish, or some combo of the three') or because of his rape jokes and snipes about feminism. He also had a record of opposing certain reproductive rights for women, suggesting that society should 'claim a right and an interest' in the fate of the unborn child and therefore might limit abortion access to any woman who 'is the victim of rape or incest, or if her mental or physical health is threatened' as part of an 'historic compromise' offering in return a health service with free contraception and an adoption service.

Thus Hitchens urged that the state should be involved in adjudicating the specific rights and wrongs of individual abortion cases. And, if he conceded that, in some circumstances, abortion might be justified, his celebration of the abortion by nature of 'deformed or idiot children who would otherwise have been born' indicates certain unnerving normative criteria about just who might be considered candidates for future members of the human race. Drawing a parallel with evolution, he suggested that 'the system' was 'fairly pitiless in eliminating those who never had a very good chance of surviving in the first place'.[32] It is hard to detect in this a moral position on abortion qualitatively superior to that of the Reverend Falwell.

The overall thrust of Hitchens's work on religion, then, was to pin on it social evils that are the product of a much more complex set of determinations. And, given the way he treated religion as a set of static ideas embedded in a body of texts, with a clearly immanent and literal meaning, this cannot but be seen as reverting to an idealist position. Hitchens maintained that God was the product of human beings, but the writer was not consistent with the implications of this argument. One such implication is that religion is a labour of interpretation, of symbolic and ideological production from which agents derive meanings adequate to their life circumstances. Apart from anything else, the sheer indeterminacy of religious texts would make it impossible for there to be a literal, consistent meaning present in the texts: interpretation is indispensable. And if we are to take the materialist approach that Hitchens purported to defend, such interpretation must have reference to the contemporary social conditions and antagonisms in which people find themselves.

The shortcomings in Hitchens's approach to religion were evident long ago. In an early essay on religion, 'The Lord and the Intellectuals', Hitchens took issue with the growing profile of religion in American politics and sought to defend what he characterised as a Marxist reading:

Many of the radical clergy of our own time seem almost haggard in their effort to prove, by their own shiningly political example, that Marx was being unfair in dismissing religion as the opium of the people. Pity for them that their understanding of Marx is as muddled as their under-standing of the Bible. What he said was this:

> Religious distress is at the same time the expression of real distress and the protest against real distress. Religion is the sigh of the oppressed creature, the heart of the heartless world, just as it is the spirit of a spiritless situation. It is the opium of the people. The demand to give up the illusions about its conditions is the demand to give up a condition that needs illusions. Criticism has plucked the imaginary flowers from the chain not so that men will wear the chain without any fantasy or consolation but so that they will break the chain and cull the living flower. (Critique of Hegel's *Philosophy of Right*)

> What is being argued in this passage is not that religious enthusiasts and prophets are dope peddlers. That is the universal vulgarization of Marx's opinion. What Marx meant is that there is a chord of credulity waiting to be struck in all of us. It is most likely to be struck successfully if the stroke comes concealed as an argument for moral and humane behavior.[33]

This, bewilderingly, rebuts one vulgarisation with another. It is a mis-reading bordering on travesty to say that Marx's passage here adverted to a 'chord of credulity' (meaning, I suppose, an innate need for some transcendent experience, which religion purports to supply). It is quite correct that Marx was not dismissing religion in this passage but rather ascribing its power to earthly sources, or what Marxists describe as the 'material conditions' of exploitation and oppression. Hitchens, as he made clear during the Rushdie affair, did not agree with this approach. Religion had 'a life of its own', and by the time of the war on terror had assumed such gigantic proportions in Hitchens's mind that it explained almost everything. God is not great? Hard to believe after such a lengthy tribute to his puissance.

DOMINIONS, HEAVENLY AND IMPERIAL

'Most irritating of all', Hitchens had complained in the 1980s,

> there are still people on the left who say feebly that, 'after all, there are so many "progressive" church people. Look at the Maryknolls or Arch-bishop Romero.' This is usually said by people who are not themselves religious but who feel that religion is good enough for other people – usually other people in the Third World … I'm thinking here of pathetic oxymorons like 'Liberty Baptist' or 'Liberation Theology.'[34]

Hitchens was always impatient with the idea that the religious might be able to interpret their doctrine in ways that facilitated their liberation – there could be no coexistence between liberty and religion.

Still, Hitchens's mind harboured a certain hierarchy of superstition, such that the religion of the colonialists certainly outranked the ideas of colonial subjects. 'Missionary Christianity', he pointed out, 'often maintained that, by codifying and ritualizing primitive magic, it civilized paganism and witchcraft.' This was, as far as Hitchens was concerned, 'a fair claim'.[35] And like many of the new atheists whom he would go on to call his allies, he would find that Islam was, among religions, the worst. For Hitchens Islam was a malady consisting of a triumvirate of 'self-righteousness, self-pity, and self-hatred – the self-righteousness dating from the seventh century, the self-pity from the 13th (when the "last" Caliph was kicked to death in Baghdad by the Mongol warlord Hulagu), and the self-hatred from the 20th'.[36]

'It took me a long time', Hitchens suggested, 'to separate and classify' these 'three now-distinctive elements of the new and grievance-privileged Islamist mentality'.[37] One hopes this was stage humility. The thought that this pithy trinity was the result of years of painstaking and laborious assay on Hitchens's part is not a little insulting to the author.

Hitchens's obsession with the furies of Islam obviously arose from the need to supply an analysis for Islamist attacks on the United States that did not include actual US foreign policy as part of the explanation. Thus, responding to claims that US foreign policy had motivated the attacks, Hitchens expostulated that

> the grievance and animosity predate even the Balfour Declaration, let alone the occupation of the West Bank. They predate the creation of Iraq as a state. The gates of Vienna would have had to fall to the Ottoman jihad before any balm could begin to be applied to these psychic wounds.[38]

Likewise, he would not have it said by anyone that suicide attacks in Israel or in Iraq or elsewhere had anything to do with anything but 'evil mullahs' with their 'evil preaching' and 'vile religion'.[39]

In other words this was not a conflict generated by contemporary conditions but rather more fundamentally by the genetic structure of Islam itself. His attack on Islam was two-pronged. He demanded on the one hand that it undergo a reformation and declared that if it could not do so, there could be no coexistence with Islam. On the other hand, having said this, he insisted that Islam could not have a reformation:

If you ask specifically what is wrong with Islam, it makes the same mistakes as the preceding religions, but it makes another mistake, which is that it's unalterable. You notice how liberals keep saying, 'If only Islam would have a Reformation' – it can't have one. It says it can't. It's extremely dangerous in that way.[40]

The historical record indicates that Islam has been as changeable as any other religion and that the last two centuries have witnessed the most striking reformations. Indeed, the origins of Islamism are in precisely an attempt to reform Islam, to render it adequate to the challenge posed by the colonial invasion, dislocation, and subjugation of Muslim societies. There were, of course, fundamentalist variants, such as Wahabbism, that purported to revere a true Islam and thus promised to regenerate declining Muslim societies. But modernising tendencies also appeared in sections of the Ottoman Empire, using the interpretive techniques of *itjihad* to derive Islamic doctrines appropriate for capitalist modernity or at least capable of meeting its challenge. Contemporary 'political Islam' derives its original force from this tendency.[41] So Hitchens's charge was historically illiterate and missed the point of what he was raging against.

The result of this sequence of vulgarisations and misconceptions was that Hitchens endorsed the neoconservative Mark Steyn's claim that Muslims constitute a demographic threat to Europe, and Hitchens defended his friend Martin Amis when the latter confessed to a desire to subject Muslims to

not letting them travel. Deportation – further down the road. Curtailing of freedoms. Strip-searching people who look like they're from the Middle East or from Pakistan ... Discriminatory stuff, until it hurts the whole community and they start getting tough with their children.

Countering what he called Sam Harris's irresponsible argument, that fascists were the sole repository of good sense in respect to the Islamic threat, Hitchens boasted: 'Not while I'm alive, they won't [be]'.[42]

Naturally, Hitchens always denied that there could be such a thing as anti-Muslim racism, or Islamophobia. He pronounced it a dumb word that failed to comprehend that belief was a matter of choice. 'A stupid term – Islamophobia – has been put into circulation to try and suggest that a foul prejudice lurks behind any misgivings about Islam's infallible "message"', he complained. This term was being used to berate 'the civilized world', which was guilty of none of the horrors of the Muslim world – a complaint that steps nimbly around the entire history of colonialism and imperialism, of course.[43]

It would surely be unsporting to deprive people such as Hitchens of their misgivings about Islam, but the definition of *Islamophobia* has nothing to do with simple quibbles, doubts, or criticisms of the faith. Here are some of the elements of Islamophobia as identified by the Runnymede Trust, a British think tank that focuses on race. Islamophobia treats Islam 'as a monolithic bloc, static and unresponsive to change', 'as separate and "other"', 'as inferior to the West', 'as violent, aggressive, threatening, supportive of terrorism and engaged in a "clash of civilisations"'.[44] Each of these points alights on a specific, central feature of racism: essentialist thinking, ascriptive denigration, supremacism, and demonology. What is more, on each of these points, Hitchens must be judged an Islamophobe. Nor is it possible to rescue Hitchens's position by saying that Islam is merely a voluntary belief. If Hitchens knew, as he frequently said, that race itself was a construct, there is no reason why it must be constructed solely out of somatic materials; the history of racism is littered with cultural, religious, and national chauvinisms.

It is only logical – dare I say, predictable? – that Hitchens should have developed this chauvinist streak while batting for empire. His ferocious American nationalism required that the Islamists be portrayed as symbolic rivals to the US on a par with the late USSR. Since the Islamists are scattered, politically diverse, and militarily feeble opponents, and since many are actually in alliance with the US, the ideological work necessary to make this into a coherent threat was considerable. These disarticulated groups and movements had to be somehow sutured and also linked to a wider series of supposed threats (cultural, demographic, etc.). And the point at which they could be thus articulated was through their supposed common foundation in a changeless doctrine of Islam, the ideal-essence animating a world-historic conflict between civilisations. So it is to this imperialist nationalism, its lineaments and roots, that I now turn.

4 THE ENGLISHMAN ABROAD AND THE ROAD TO EMPIRE

In the end, the liberals always do what the empire wants.

– Christopher Hitchens, *Nation*

Do I think our civilisation is superior? Yes, I do. Do I think it's worth fighting for? Most certainly.

– Christopher Hitchens, *Guardian*

ANGLO-AMERICAN IRONIES

Hitchens's fascination with the United States is traceable to his earliest childhood. Memories of brash, grinning Americans 'over here' – 'so large, so friendly, and so rich' – formed the elemental psychic fuel of this enthrallment. America seemed 'either too modern', without history, or 'simply too premodern', with its barren frontiers; 'at once the most conservative and commercial AND the most revolutionary society on earth'.[1] For a provincial Englander it was also vast in promise. Along with his belatedly discovered Jewish heritage, his American self formed part of a compound identity for Hitchens – one sufficiently singular as to distinguish him among his peers but not so exotic as to be a career impediment.

Throughout his years at Oxford, he had known Americans and yearned to know America. He had watched the moon landing, yawped with delight when the Stars and Stripes were placed on the 'silvery orb', and thrilled with what in retrospect he realised was a latent American patriotism. Or, at least, this is how he wanted it to be recorded. His comrades from the time do not recall any utterances that could have given rise to a suspicion of such patriotism, but this most likely reflects Hitchens's adeptness at keeping certain aspects of himself tactfully hidden.[2]

At Balliol he applied for a scholarship to visit the United States. This experience gave him 'a sharply new picture of life in the United States'. He saw New York City, 'redolent of sex'; the women of Chicago 'en fête' at a feminist rally in all their 'bird-of-paradise variety'; and declared the Bay Area seductive. Young American women were 'more ... forward'. The whole country was humming with activity, and it seemed 'a state of affairs worth fighting for, or at least fighting over'. He returned repeatedly. What he most liked was that 'here in the USA it seemed to be true that if you dared to give things "your best shot" then the other much-used phrases like "land of opportunity" would kick in as well'.[3] Finally, in October 1981 he left Heathrow with a one-way ticket to New York, the promise of a flat, and a potential job at the *Nation* magazine. He had a lot to be patriotic about.

And despite his criticisms of American society and particularly the 'ruling class crime wave' carried out under the Reaganite junta, his patriotism would habitually come through. It would express itself, for example, during the Columbus Day celebrations in 1992, when he lauded the accomplishments of the Indian wars. 1492 was 'a very good year', he argued, equivalent to the great progressive leap of the Roman conquest of the British mainland. While it was not always the case, it was generally true, 'as Marx wrote about India' (*sic*), that 'the impact of a more developed society upon a culture (or a series of warring cultures, since there was no such nation as India before the British Empire) can spread aspects of modernity and enlightenment that outlive and transcend the conqueror'. However:

> Those who view the history of North America as a narrative of genocide and slavery are, it seems to me, hopelessly stuck on this reactionary position. They can think of the Western expansion of the United States only in terms of plague blankets, bootleg booze and dead buffalo, never in terms of the medicine chest, the wheel and the railway. One need not be an automatic positivist about this. But it does happen to be the way that history is made, and to complain about it is as empty as complaint about climatic, geological or tectonic shift ... The transformation of part of the northern part of this continent into 'America' inaugurated a nearly boundless epoch of opportunity and innovation, and thus deserves to be celebrated with great vim and gusto.[4]

The historian David Stannard derided this view as 'quasi-Hitlerian', 'vulgar social Darwinism', involving 'precisely the same sort of retrospective justifications for genocide that would have been offered by the descendants of Nazi storm troopers and SS doctors had the Third Reich ultimately had its way'.[5] This adverts to the manner in which the ideologies of social Darwinism that flourished at the zenith of colonialism later formed the basis of fascist ideology. But if Hitchens was partaking of a rebarbative logic with a despicable pedigree, he was doing so for reasons of his own peculiar version of progress. As I mentioned earlier, this is one of the things he meant by Marxism. Alexander Cockburn, Hitchens's former comrade and one-time paragon, suggested that Hitchens

> was on a trajectory toward this for quite a long time. He has always had this crude Marxist stageist view of history, and he now applies this to Iraq – so the 'Islamofascists' have to give way to secular, historically progressive forces that the US supposedly represents.[6]

On this basis Hitchens would go on to complain bitterly that the left had never thought America 'a good idea to begin with'.[7]

Yet, for all this, Hitchens remained an opponent of US foreign policy for a long time. The remarkable shifts in his position as he traversed the 1990s are indicative of an attempt to resolve the antagonism between his desire to remain on the left and his desire to see the US as a 'good idea'.

FROM DESERT STORM TO YUGOSLAVIA

During the reign of Bush the Elder, Hitchens was able to be anti-imperialist for the most part without ambiguity. He did not care for the president and rejected his policy; this was straightforward. Hitchens had been an outstanding critic of Desert Storm.

The cynicism of America's various tilts in the Gulf region could hardly be justified on the humanitarian grounds confected by Hill & Knowlton. This was an exercise, Hitchens decided, in realpolitik: a 'Metternich of Arabia' followed by a freemasonry of 'shady oilmen'. America had encouraged Saddam in his worst days and backed the Iranian regime at the same time in order to maintain a balance. Hitchens pointed out that America's signals to the Iraqi regime through April Glaspie had encouraged Hussein to believe that he would be welcome to Kuwait (Glaspie later claimed that they had not expected him to take *all* of Kuwait) and suggested that a tilt towards the Saudi regime, with a protective 'net of bases and garrisons' thrown over it, could have its own destabilising potential.

US policy was undermining democratic and secular forces, making further wars more likely. Hitchens would have none of the Churchillian rhetoric either: 'Beware always of the Munich/Churchill rhetoric, as of the ignorant opportunists who make use of it.' About liberals who 'pronounced themselves co-belligerents', preferring 'imperialism to fascism', he suggested: 'Now with a ruined Iraq and a strengthened Saddam – not to mention a strengthened Al-Saud and Al-Sabah – we no longer have to choose between imperialism and fascism.'[8]

Writing of atrocities committed against fleeing Iraqi troops, he looked forward to 'the editions of *Sesame Street* and other special programming in place of cartoon fare in which American children will have the turkey shoot explained to them'. The new world order, as Bush Sr. called it, inaugurated a period of

> direct engagement and permanent physical presence. Moments like this are traditionally marked by some condign lesson being meted out to the locals. The fantastic, exemplary bloodletting that took place after the ostensible issue of the conflict had been decided was in that tradition. I can hardly wait for the parades.[9]

Nor was his eloquence restricted to his writing. In debate with Morton Kondracke, a senior editor of the *New Republic* and a neoconservative who strongly supported the war, Hitchens fumed that Iraq was being sacrificed to empire. War had 'been made *en masse* on civilians they can't bury fast enough'. Even the 'principal moral author' of the Bush administration's propaganda of a war for democracy, Kanan Makiya, had described Baghdad as, in Hitchens's paraphrase, 'a city from which human life has been taken out. The water doesn't run, the electricity doesn't run, the hospitals are finished, the schools closed, the bodies unburied in the streets.' Further,

> the United Nations report … says that the conditions are 'apocalyptic' … there are four horsemen if you remember. The two still to come, naturally created by a bombing campaign that takes out the reservoirs, that takes out the sewage, that takes out the hospitals and the electricity: famine and pestilence. Those are next.

All this was for no nobler purpose than the effective management of American proxies:

If we define Saddam as a weakened, crippled 'Hitler', haven't we got more or less the definition of the ideal client? Isn't this the sort of guy we've always wanted? … Unlike the British empire and the French empire which it's replacing in the region, the American hasn't until recently ruled by direct physical presence, it's ruled by proxy: Israel, Saudi Arabia, Iran, Turkey. In order, then: the Israelis wouldn't mind a Lebanised Iraq. They didn't mind a Lebanised Lebanon if it came to that. They wouldn't mind a Lebanised Middle East. They want to take other countries' nationalist challengers off the chessboard. Who wouldn't? If they want a 'Greater Israel', they'll need to do that. Why you should pay for this is a question I don't know whether you ever ask yourself … you are paying for it, anyway, so you should ask … The Saudis don't want that, Saudi Arabia doesn't need a Lebanised Iraq on its border. So it's against. Big argument in Washington politics between the Saudi faction of the government and the Israeli faction … Thus, I think I have aptly described to you the situation among your imperial proxies. While they squabble, Iraq dies. Dies. And reverts to barbarism and strife and misery and disease, and tries to bury its dead. And this is what it is to have an empire.[10]

Two facts about Hitchens's arguments are striking. The first is that despite the advantage they had over their rivals' on the prowar side, they expressed, in an idiom that he would have described as Marxist, a relatively conventional left-Realist analysis of international relations. The second was the evincive passion of his position. As I have argued, Hitchens had a remarkable gift for mobilising sentiment, and he did so here with aplomb. Perhaps it is a tribute to the rhetorical power of these performances that, when asked about this period of his writing after some of it was quoted in Tariq Ali's *Bush in Babylon*, Hitchens replied, 'All I felt was, I can't imagine writing like that anymore.'[11]

In 1992, however, two events created a contradiction for Hitchens that was not resolved until 9/11: the election of Bill Clinton, whom he loathed, and the beginning of war in Bosnia, which increasingly, Hitchens thought, demanded some form of US intervention. In retrospect Hitchens attempted to confer on his position more consistency than it actually possessed. As he explained in 2004:

It starts for me at the end of the first Gulf War, the one in 1991, which I was very critical of until the closing stages, when I was in Northern Iraq bouncing around in a jeep with some Kurdish guerrillas. They taped a picture of George Bush senior to their windshield, on my side, so that

I couldn't see out. And after a bit I complained. I said 'look do we have to have this, I can't see' (and also it would be awfully embarrassing if I ran into anyone I knew). I remember that the Iran-Contra business was very vivid in my mind. They said 'the fact of the matter is we can move it to a side window if you like, but we think that without his intervention, without the umbrella in Northern Iraq, that we, and all our families, would be dead'. And I realised that I didn't have a clever answer to that. And I began to re-work back to the origins of the war and realised that co-existence with the Saddam Hussein regime was no longer possible. And that was in 1991. Anyway, if you hadn't concluded it by then you were obviously not going to be persuaded – as since we have found out.[12]

This story lends Hitchens's position not only consistency but a superficial moral plausibility. Who could speak more eloquently about Saddam's repression and the best means of opposing it than the surviving victims of his genocidal outrages? Who else could turn an imperialist war into a necessary humanitarian war? Yet it is not reflected in Hitchens's writing in 1991 – or after, as I will show. Nor does it concur with the recollection of his friends. The writer and comedian Dennis Perrin, who knew Hitchens in this period, recalls:

He never stopped criticizing Bush's 'mad contest' with Saddam, much less opined that 'co-existence' with Saddam was 'no longer possible'. I have a tape of him debating Ken Adelman on C-SPAN in 1993 where he's still critical of the Gulf War, and again no mention of wanting to overthrow Saddam. As late as 2002, when I asked him directly if he did indeed favor a US invasion, he waffled and said that W. would have to convince him on 'about a zillion fronts' before he could sign on.[13]

The same can be said for Hitchens's writing on Yugoslavia, where he initially and for some time opposed any idea of a US bombing campaign on behalf of Bosnia. Hitchens's resistance to the prowar conclusion, which he eventually reached, is all the more arresting since he predicated much of his journalism in this period on the premise that Serbia, under the leadership of Slobodan Milosevic, was conspiring to destroy Yugoslavia as a multinational state and annex as much territory as possible into a 'Greater Serbia'.

I will not rehearse the history of Yugoslavia's breakup here, but it is necessary to underline the extent to which Hitchens's position was what his close companion Martin Amis would describe as 'moral-visceral' – and to that extent a mystification. Like the great majority of Anglophone writing on Yugoslavia, Hitchens's journalism laid the stress on demonology, on identifying a single Balkan villain against whom a needful victim could be defined. Whereas for most commentators the template was World War II, for Hitchens the correct analogy was the Spanish Civil War, with Bosnia a plucky, pluralist, multicultural republic to Serbia's nationalists.

The problem with such a stance was that a certain amount of political and moral blindness was a compulsory accompaniment. For example, one noticed Serb camps like Trnopolje or Omarska but not Bugojno or Orašac, which were run by the Bosnian army and the sites of serious abuses. One saw the atrocities of Republika Srpska, and occasionally those of the Croatian government, but not those of General Naser Oric and the Bosnian army. This is not to imply parity: the Serb forces were by far the most powerful, and the share of total civilian deaths attributed to their actions reflects this. But it is to suggest that Hitchens's tendency to idealise those whom he had chosen as allies or heroes meant a sacrifice of critical faculties, of probity. The Bosnian leadership was not a faction of beleaguered democratic dissidents, innocent of nationalist realpolitik and brutality, as he liked to pretend. It is also to suggest that skimming along the representational surface of the Anglophone media, without investigating the real causes and dynamics of the conflict, left Hitchens in need of an ideological stopgap whenever historical explanation was required. The anti-Serb demonology fit the bill.[14] In the long term this stance proved incompatible with an anti-imperialist position, and Hitchens struggled on this account to develop an explanation of US actions in the Balkans consistent with his left-realism – with the result of a collapse into the liberal imperialism that he had once castigated.

Still, as late as March 1993, Hitchens averred that he was a 'convinced anti-interventionist, who would not wish to see the Bosnians go the way of the Kurds in some "Balkan Storm" foolishness'. He supported only 'the universal demand' of Bosnians, which was 'for an end to the arms embargo, which in practice is an intervention on the side of the well-accoutred Serbian expansionists'. He went on to acknowledge that Croatia's HDZ regime had 'expelled tens of thousands of Serbs and defined the remainder as aliens in their own country', describing this as an 'outrage to Serbian and Russian sensibilities'. He called for 'a serious plan to help the defenceless Republic of Bosnia and Herzegovina to preserve what remains of its multicultural and democratic character', which would require an extraordinary effort on the part of everyone who still believes in internationalism. It will have to confront the exhausted amorality of the imperial mapmakers like Lord Owen, and also the opportunism of certain Islamic fundamentalists who are looking for an easy opening. It will have to confront the Croatian as well as the Serbian irredentists, and extend a hand to the democratic opposition in Serbia itself. It will also, in calling for the embargo to be lifted, end up calling for it to be broken.[15]

Again, in June 1993, it remained a question of calling for an end to the arms embargo, not for US military intervention. Citing a statement from Dr Haris Silajdzic, the Bosnian foreign minister, calling for the withdrawal of UN peacekeeping troops, Hitchens wondered that 'a nation that is fighting for survival actually demands to be left alone to fight its own battles'. But a note of impatience was beginning to creep into his despatches, particularly with 'the many liberals and pacifists who have been worrying themselves sick about "another Vietnam" and the renowned American propensity for violence'. 'Relax, Erwin Knoll and *The Progressive*,' he said. 'Lighten up, Barbara Ehrenreich … Chill out, Ronald Steel and Eric Alterman. With Bill at the helm, you are in safe hands.'[16]

By 1994 Hitchens was prepared to argue that while the Gulf War, 'an imperialist war, par excellence' had no moral case in its favour, the Kurdish protectorate in northern Iraq – covered by a no-fly zone – had 'demonstrated that enlightened pressure can to some extent help to redeploy military force, for defensible purposes, in an intelligent and limited way'.[17] He also cast a wary eye on the arguments and activities of his old comrades in the Socialist Workers' Party whose story, he held, was unmistakably one of decline since his departure, exemplified in its argument that the war in Bosnia was a civil war led on all sides by unappealing nationalists with few democratic credentials.[18] However, this did not yet signal a stabilisation of Hitchens's position on the side of imperialism.

When the United States led another series of air attacks on Yugoslavia under NATO command, ostensibly to end a wave of ethnic cleansing against Kosovo Albanians, Hitchens's first reflex was once again to distrust the exercise. While he was later to deploy the increasingly familiar line that 'if the counsel of the peaceniks had been followed' something dreadful would have happened, he was initially far less sanguine about the American strikes. Dennis Perrin recalls that Hitchens opposed attacks on Serbia. I remember because I asked him directly. He said no. Then, one day, he was for it. Lots of it … his hatred of Bill Clinton coincided with his support of Clinton's attack. It was the kind of 'contradiction', one of Hitchens's favourite words, that he revelled in.[19]

This description is confirmed by a glance at Hitchens's writing on Kosovo. In the early weeks of the war, he was scornful of attempts by the war leaders to justify the war retrospectively in light of the ethnic cleansing that took place during the war. 'The cleansing interval', he pointed out, '… was both provoked and provided by the threat of air attacks on other parts of Yugoslavia'. About the responsibility of the warmongers for the fate of Kosovars, he added:

> The 'line of the day' among administration spokesmen, confronted by the masses of destitute and terrified refugees and solid reports of the mass execution of civilians, [was] to say that 'we expected this to happen' … If they want to avoid being indicted for war crimes themselves, these 'spokesmen' had better promise us they were lying when they said that.[20]

Again, in May, he extensively documented statements from the White House and Pentagon, describing how they had anticipated and even allowed for ethnic cleansing to take place: it was part of their war plans. 'If this mass expulsion was anticipated', Hitchens averred, 'and if the deliberate response was the bombing of urban targets well outside the borders of Kosovo, then our leaders belong in the dock also.'[21] This was Hitchens's consistent argument: NATO leaders were war criminals who had precipitated needless suffering and were engaging in 'a carve-up' with the intention of in some way redividing Kosovo as part of a wider pattern of divide-and-rule tactics deployed by NATO.[22]

Nor did he, as he was to later, defend the honour of the Blair government while trashing Clinton. Instead, he pointed out the ruthless absurdity of the government's claiming to have anticipated ethnic cleansing but refusing to make humanitarian provision for it on the ground that, as Clare Short put it, 'It would have been an appalling act of complicity in ethnic cleansing to set up in advance a network of camps.'[23] Was it not, he wondered, 'even more cynical – more complicitous to have left these people on the hillsides?' Most significantly, perhaps, Hitchens still anticipated an imperial redivision, which he argued necessitated ethnic cleansing:

Somewhere at the back of NATO's mind there is a project for the partition and amputation of Kosovo, and nobody who has studied the partitions of Ireland, India, Cyprus, Palestine and Bosnia can believe for an instant that partition can be accomplished without ethnic cleansing.

This is the third sweep of massacre and displacement to have convulsed the region since 1992. During the first and nastiest the rape and carnage that emptied much of Bosnia and Herzegovina of Muslims, and was conducted by Serbian and Croatian fascists acting in collusion – NATO played the role of non-neutral spectator by imposing an arms embargo on Bosnian self-defense. During the second – the 1995 removal of all Serbs from their ancestral places in the 'Krajina', or borderland, of Croatia the muscle and training for the operation was actually supplied by a consortium of US military men with the full knowledge and consent of Washington. (The International Criminal Tribunal is now seeking the arrest of some of their Croatian underlings, who did the routine killing and burning.) I noticed at the time that Milosevic kept almost eerily quiet about this atrocity and that he deployed almost no force to try to prevent or reverse it. The reason, as I swiftly learned, was that he had a use for the Serb refugees. They were to be warehoused in various slums and camps until they could be moved – to Kosovo. If I could know that, so could NATO.[24]

This analysis takes to its very limit the position of opposing imperialist intervention while simultaneously accepting the worst possible case against Slobodan Milosevic. In retrospect it seems bizarre. There was probably never any doubt that a sort of protocolonial autonomy (that is, independence from Serbia, dependence on NATO and the United Nations) would descend on Kosovo. The idea that the prosecutors of the war were secretly contriving to engineer a partition of Kosovo as part of a long-term master plan to partition Yugoslavia was far too dependent on each of its premises' being true. One false premise and the whole argument collapses.

For example, should it turn out to be incorrect that Milosevic had his own blueprint to transfer Serbs ethnically cleansed from Krajina under aegis of 'Operation Storm' to slums in Kosovo, and that this alone explained his failure to detach units of the Yugoslav People's Army to prevent the expulsions, then a crucial limb in any US plan would be missing. And what if the arms embargo Hitchens claimed was imposed by NATO (in fact by the United Nations) was actually broken by the leading NATO power, the US, enabling waves of armed mujahedeen fighters to be helicoptered into Bosnia as, indeed, Hitchens knew it was? In this case would not the idea of NATO's being a calculating foe of the Bosnian military leadership at least be in need of some nuance? Hitchens's argument against intervention relied on absurd assumptions. As such it was susceptible to collapse when refuted by reality. This must, however, at least be qualified by one observation: that the intervening powers had in fact acted to accelerate the partition of Yugoslavia, that the charge made about US complicity in Operation Storm was substantially accurate, and that Kosovo would go on to be both annexed and partitioned in a sense – just not in the way that Hitchens foresaw. Ultimately, the weaknesses in Hitchens's position derived from the incompatibility between opposition to US intervention on the one hand and the overestimation of the Bosnian leadership, combined with the demonisation of the Serbian leadership, on the other.[25]

Hitchens later began to make a radically different argument, albeit one that shared many of the same premises concerning the singular, lunatic predilections of Slobodan Milosevic. Reproaching those on the left whom he saw as revisionists, Hitchens argued,

> The NATO intervention repatriated all or most of the refugees and killed at least some of the cleansers. I find I have absolutely no problem with that. It's nothing when compared with the disgrace of having once been Milosevic's partner in peace.

Further, Hitchens argued that the act of having intervened, and of having given the humanitarian reasons the US did, compelled the US to act again on humanitarian grounds and save East Timor from the genocidal depredations of Indonesian military forces. There appeared to be 'a new era' afoot, in which the 'old reflexes serve us less well'. Since 'traditional interventionists like Henry Kissinger' were opposed to humanitarian interventions, it was doubtful whether they were 'mere power-projection for the New World Order'. The responsibility of the left in this situation was to always 'take the side of the victims'. And so:

> I support military resistance to Serbian racism and aggression and the landing of Australian and other troops in East Timor, and if it were up to me, both of these decisions would have been taken earlier (with correspondingly large savings on the humanitarian catastrophe account).[26]

The problem with Hitchens's argument now was that he had provided no account of how taking 'the side of the victims' had come to result in such different conclusions on his part. Something was unsettling, even disturbing, about his ability to swerve from one position to its opposite in such a short interval without acknowledging any requirement for explanation. How did he no longer notice, or care, that the war had knowingly produced a mass exodus of refugees? How could he forget what he once knew, namely, that 'the cleansers' were the least of the victims of NATO's bombing? By what route did he come by the view that Prime Minister Blair, whose government Hitchens had interrogated for its seeming cynicism and complicity in ethnic cleansing, was acting out of principle? How was Clinton a war criminal for having bombed El-Shifa and sites in Afghanistan, but somehow putting up military resistance to Serbian ultranationalism and aggression in Yugoslavia?[27]

As Hitchens moved on to his next major venture, *The Trial of Henry Kissinger*, it was clear that he was not wholly reconciled to US imperialism. But it was also clear from the way he used Kissinger's name and reputation that it served largely as a negative benchmark against which interventions conducted under the rubric of 'human rights' could be justified: 'It is not a Kissinger policy' became a seal of approval in itself.

In fact, the sheer immensity of evil condensed in Kissingerian imperialism allowed one to relativise not only about humanitarian imperialism but also some crimes committed in what might be called a Kissingerian context. In May 2001 there was widespread discussion of former senator Bob Kerrey's participation in the Thanh Phong massacre, in which a Vietnamese peasant family consisting of an elderly man, a woman, and children younger than twelve were stabbed to death with knives. Hitchens, asked about the subject on Fox News, reminded viewers that Kerrey was the president of the New School, where Hitchens taught, before adding a relativising defence:

> None of the people he killed were raped. None of them were dismembered. None of them were tortured. None of them were mutilated, had their ears cut off. He never referred to them as gooks or slopes or afterwards. So … for one day's work in a free-fire zone in the Mekong Delta, it was nothing like as bad as most days.[28]

One can imagine a similar act by a soldier-cum-politician whom Hitchens loathed – say, if he was from Belgrade rather than Nebraska – and the volume of bile that he would have unloaded on anyone offering such a defence. There might have been no abrupt transformation in Hitchens's affiliations had there been no 11 September 2001. But a context for his reversal had already been established. He had begun to identify the United States Armed Forces as a human rights detachment, an antigenocide task force, and a vector for democracy.

'MY COUNTRY AFTER ALL'

'Watching the towers fall in New York', Hitchens told David Horowitz's *Frontpage* magazine in 2003,

> with civilians incinerated on the planes and in the buildings, I felt something that I couldn't analyze at first and didn't fully grasp … I am only slightly embarrassed to tell you that this was a feeling of exhilaration. Here we are then, I was thinking, in a war to the finish between everything I love and everything I hate. Fine. We will win and they will lose. A pity that we let them pick the time and place of the challenge, but we can and we will make up for that.

As he later affirmed, 'a whole new terrain of struggle had just opened up in front of me.' Recalling 'the title of that Orwell essay from 1940 … "My Country Right or Left"', he thought about the USA: '*My country after all.*' So, 'shall I take out the papers of citizenship?' Hitchens asked, heart taking wing like a passenger jet. 'Wrong question. In every essential way, I already have.'[29]

In retrospect Hitchens represented his view as a fairly consistent one: from the day of the concremation, he recognised a world-historic conflict between secular progress and religious reaction, and he took his side. He would go on to lambast the left for the poverty of its instinctive reaction, which he characterised as a desire to 'sit out' or take a neutral stand in the combat between the United States and al-Qaeda, a preference that the problem had not 'come up' so that liberals could continue with their 'domestic agenda'. In fact, his knee did not jerk immediately in the way that this macho taunt might suggest. His initial stance was far more cautious. His friend Dennis Perrin recalls:

> Just after the attack, I believe [he] was on the West Coast, and he counselled calm and reflection. That didn't last very long. By the time of his 'Against Rationalization' in *The Nation*, it was clear he was taking this all the way.

And this is borne out in his early postconflagration articles, which mocked John McCain's suggestion that the attacks be deemed 'an act of war', mocked Bush for the same rhetoric, and conveyed alarm that it seemed so difficult to ask 'if the United States has ever done anything to attract such awful hatred' – 'the analytical moment, if there is to be one, has been indefinitely postponed'.[30] And so, in Hitchens's case, it was. Within a week he was charging that such analytical thoughts constituted a form of rationalisation.

The viciousness with which he attacked former comrades in print was exceeded only by his private vindictiveness. His former colleague at the *Nation*, Sam Husseini, had made the mistake of disputing Hitchens's 'Against Rationalization' piece announcing his break from the Left with analysis of the type that would once have been a mainstay of Hitchens's columns, by suggesting that al-Qaeda would be starved for recruits were it not for manifest injustices perpetrated by the US government. In print Hitchens retorted: 'If Husseini knows what was in the minds of the murderers, it is his solemn responsibility to inform us of the source of his information, and also to share it with the authorities.' Yet, by this rationale, anyone who attempted an explanation for the atrocities that went beyond the obvious facts of 'how' – that is, anyone who attempted an *analysis* – was claiming inside knowledge. In correspondence Hitchens told Husseini:

> I am dead serious about my first point and will call you on it again. If you claim you knew what these people had in mind, I want you to show me that you contacted the authorities with your information before you sent your blithering little letter to me. Either that or you shut the fuck up – not that it matters any more what you say. And you claim to know how enemies are made … You have no idea.[31]

If it seemed that there was something, as Hitchens liked to say, *minatory* about the article, this missive was openly threatening.

An abrupt change occurred not just in Hitchens's tone but in his authorial voice. Hitchens emerged a convinced American nationalist, deploying its full tonal diapason – from hysteria to triumphalism, with the scale calibrated by braggadocio. His lexicon was updated accordingly, as he discovered the utility of words such as *terrorism*, *evil*, and *anti-American*. To each of these terms, which he had previously rejected, he devoted at least one article by way of rehabilitation. Later the old Cold War lexicon of totalitarianism availed itself to him as he turned his attention to religion. A lugubrious, sentimental timbre crept into some of his writing, abated only by the energy with which he prosecuted the war on the left.

It was one thing to emote about 'the almost-eclipsed figure of the American proletarian, who was busting his sinews in the rubble and carnage of downtown while the more refined elements wrung their hands'.[32] But Hitchens was even more lachrymose about the felled towers themselves. Not a 'Rockefeller boondoggle ... massively subsidised by public sector tenants', as his former colleague Mike Davis had suggested, the World Trade Center 'looked down quite benignly on a neighbourhood, a district, a quarter, where each language had a chance'. Hitchens recalled migrating by train from New York to DC, and

> I ... twisted around in my seat, like a child leaving a seaside holiday, until I could see the Twin Towers no more ... and every time I came back on a train or plane or by car, it was the big friendly commercial twins that signalled my return. Now each of them has met its own evil twin.

On the basis of this and similar sentimental reflections on his fondness for New York, he declared his new creed: 'Call it a rooted cosmopolitanism,' he said of his newfound nationalism, the parochial universalism of empire. 'One has to be capable of knowing when something is worth fighting for. One has to be capable of knowing an enemy when one sees one.'[33] There are many terms for this, but the mot juste is *narcissism*. The evocation of childhood, and memories of happiness watched over by the benevolent idols of finance-capitalism, obliterated by an unmentionable evil, is just a barely sublimated reflection on the author's own mortality.

Not that such sentimentality was always incompatible with the sniggering belligerence that also began to disfigure his prose. Taking advantage of an early apparent victory for the United States in Afghanistan, he taunted those who had been against Bush's war:

> Looking at some of the mind-rotting tripe that comes my way from much of today's left, I get the impression that they go to bed saying: what have I done for Saddam Hussein or good old Slobodan or the Taliban today?
>
> Well, ha ha ha, and yah, boo. It was obvious from the very start that the United States had no alternative but to do what it has done. It was also obvious that defeat was impossible ... But if, as the peaceniks like to moan, more Bin Ladens will spring up to take his place, I can offer this assurance: should that be the case, there are many many more who will

also spring up to kill him all over again. And there are more of us and we are both smarter and nicer, as well as surprisingly insistent that our culture demands respect, too.[34]

The premature triumphalism about Afghanistan needs no further criticism here, nor will I do anything to accentuate the absurdity of Hitchens's discovery that the left was in league with the enemy, but the bellicosity of the final lines cannot conceal the insecurity propelling them. This was, after all, the author who had instructed his ward, the 'young contrarian':

> Distrust any speaker who talks confidently about 'we,' or speaks in the name of 'us.' Distrust yourself if you hear these tones creeping into your own style. The search for security and majority is not always the same as solidarity; it can be another name for consensus and tyranny and tribalism.[35]

Suddenly, Hitchens could not stop talking about we and us, for there was a civilisation at stake: a tiny cult of jihadis had proved it. And no wonder, then, that he spewed so much vitriol on the left, whose dissent was tantamount to treason under such circumstances.

In fact, as the antiwar movement began to gain some traction, expanding in the most unlikely quarters of US society, Hitchens became ever more agitated and abusive. The sudden burst of dynamism did not conform to his earlier depiction of a clapped-out husk of activists long since reconciled to power but clinging to outmoded rhetoric. So, summoning his immense reserves of contumely, he let the peaceniks have it. 'The assortment of forces who assembled' on 15 February 2003, a day of coordinated worldwide protests, 'demanded, in effect, that Saddam be allowed to keep the other five-sixths of Iraq as his own personal torture chamber. There are not enough words in any idiom to describe the shame and the disgrace of this.' The protesters were divided between the silly and the sinister, the former a sentimental bunch of pacifists, the latter 'deep in their hearts' nostalgic for 'the days of the one-party State'.[36]

Not only was the left committed to a corrupt status quo internationally, but a faction of it displayed 'open sympathy for the enemies of civilization'. Cindy Sheehan was a 'LaRouchie' parroting a 'Bin Ladenist' line, Naomi Klein was writing love letters to Muqtada al-Sadr, and the *New Left Review* was entreating solidarity with Kim Il-Jong.[37] Next to such powerful indictments, and such impressive dudgeon, it would seem redundant to point out that Hitchens was dissimulating.

Klein incurred his wrath for having written intelligently, and not without a certain imaginative sympathy, about the Mahdi Army wing of the Iraqi insurgency. This amounted to swooning for 'theocratic fascists', Hitchens declared.[38] This was hardly justified. Klein by no means supported the Mahdi Army led by Muqtada al-Sadr. The article to which Hitchens objected had said,

> Muqtada al-Sadr and his followers are not just another group of generic terrorists out to kill Americans; their opposition to the occupation represents the overwhelmingly mainstream sentiment in Iraq. Yes, if elected Sadr would try to turn Iraq into a theocracy like Iran, but for now his demands are for direct elections and an end to foreign occupation.[39]

And she went on in a future piece to redouble her point that Sadr was neither an 'anti-imperialist liberator' nor 'the one-dimensional villain painted by so many in the media', the latter portrayal allowing liberals to tolerate the violent suppression of his supporters and the denial of self-government to Iraqis.[40]

But it was Cindy Sheehan, the mother of a soldier killed in Iraq, whose protest reanimated a seemingly moribund antiwar movement after the calamitous 2004 presidential election, who really aroused Hitchens's spleen. Here was a 'shifty fantasist', 'spouting sinister piffle', blaming the Iraq war on a Jewish conspiracy. The ground for this accusation was a statement attributed to Sheehan that said that her son 'was killed for lies and for a PNAC Neo-Con agenda to benefit Israel. My son joined the army to protect America, not Israel.'

Sheehan denied saying these words, but even allowing that she may have done, there is not a word about a 'Jewish cabal' in Sheehan's statement, far less anything 'LaRouche-like' in her argument. But Hitchens persisted, accusing Sheehan of 'echoing the Bin-Ladenist line that the president is the real "terrorist" and that he is the tool of a Jewish cabal'. Not just a LaRouchie, then, but also an al-Qaeda co-ideologue. Challenged about this by his former ally, Alexander Cockburn, Hitchens retreated on the LaRouchie defamation and insisted that he had not characterised Sheehan as anti-Jewish. Yet, several years on, when asked about the same incident by Brian Lamb, Hitchens again asserted that Sheehan had described the Iraq war as one fought for 'the Jewish people'. Hitchens was certainly not ignorant of the way in which such innuendo and outright slander has been used to stifle debate and not just on the question of Israel. As he wrote to Alexander Cockburn, this slander was 'often used' against those who defended the Palestinians, including himself.[41]

By this point Hitchens may simply have been incapable of rationality. The more likely diagnosis is that he had no interest in rational political conduct. In every essential way he had become a jingo.

JEFFERSONIAN BARBARISM

Having decided that he could have a patriotism that was both universalist and cosmopolitan, Hitchens also fancied that he could have imperialism without divide-and-rule, without client-states, and without the vicious massacres of the colonial era. With this in mind he set about the search for an intellectual and moral lineage and alighted on Jefferson and Paine. Had not Paine wanted America to be a superpower for democracy? Had not Jefferson fought the Barbary pirates to stop Muslim slavery?

Thus was Hitchens's new dispensation confected, as he vaunted a 'new imperialism' whose aim would be to 'enable local populations to govern themselves'. No more client-states, no more divide-and-rule, just the spread of liberal institutions as the last best hope for humanity. 'If the United States will dare to declare out loud for empire, it had better be in its capacity as a Thomas Paine arsenal, or at the very least a Jeffersonian one.'[42] As I noted in Chapter 1, the sotto voce subtext here was that, as capitalism was a revolutionary system, the only revolution left standing in fact, the freeing up of markets, coupled with the spread of liberal pluralist institutions, was itself the most progressive step available. Jeffersonian imperialism was thus neoliberal imperialism with a faint leftist patina.

Hitchens had not initially favoured an outright invasion of Iraq, but increasingly he argued there would be no war but simply a bounteous liberation, almost blood free. Soldiers would be high-fiving liberated Iraqis, distributing laptop computers and humanitarian aid to the needful subjects of Saddam. The attack would be dazzling, he fancied, and would be greeted as an emancipation – 'bring it on.'[43] However, not only was Jeffersonian imperialism exceptionally light on its feet: it was restless, expansionist, constantly looking for new destinations. Hitchens privately told his friend James Fenton that he expected Iraq to become both a protectorate of the United States and simultaneously a base from which democracy would be exported to Saudi Arabia and other regional dictatorships.[44]

But, as the occupation unravelled, seemingly disclosing new depths of depravity every day, the paeans to liberation gave way to a savage rhetoric of conquest. Hitchens's prowar arguments had always contained a great deal of scaremongering. Saddam was Hitler and Stalin combined, he said. What have we been waiting for, he wondered? Saddam has both weapons and underground chambers – just you wait. When 'just you wait' became 'never mind', Hitchens claimed he had been dispirited by the Bush administration's choosing to 'frighten people' rather than 'enlightening them'. But he had been unmistakably implicated in the administration's propaganda, not just as a member of the Committee for the Liberation of Iraq, a friend of Paul Wolfowitz's, and an ally of Ahmed Chalabi's but as a journalist.[45]

The most telling aspect of this was Hitchens's discovery of the menace of Abu Musab al-Zarqawi. Hitchens's first mention of Zarqawi was in February 2003, after Colin Powell had brought him up. The 'presence of al-Qaeda under the Iraqi umbrella is suggested chiefly by Abu Mussab al-Zarqawi, a senior bin-Laden aide and an enthusiast for chemical and biological tactics', Hitchens claimed. Meanwhile,

> most US intelligence officials now agree that it is unlikely to be a coincidence that the pro-al-Qaeda gang, Ansar al-Islam, is fighting to destroy the independent Kurdish leadership in the northern part of Iraq that has been freed from Saddam Hussein's control.

This nonsensical conspiracy theory has been amply refuted. I might mention that Zarqawi's supposed presence in Baghdad was speculation, an 'inferential leap' in the first place; both British and German intelligence cast doubt on the story at the time; even George Tenet, when testifying to a Senate committee that Zarqawi had been in Baghdad, nevertheless said that he was under the control of neither al-Qaeda nor Saddam Hussein; Zarqawi was an opponent of al-Qaeda at the time; Mullah Krekar, the Ansar al-Islam leader, denied having ever met Zarqawi and said that his group was opposed to Hussein and did not associate with al-Qaeda. Finally, according to the International Crisis Group, the potency of Ansar al-Islam was drastically inflated by the Patriotic Union of Kurdistan for its own reasons. Intelligence told a quite different story, but Hitchens had by this point dropped all pretence at serious journalism. In the end Nick Davies exposed the whole Zarqawi myth in his whistle-blowing account of the press, and showed how intelligence used the media to spread the myth.[46]

Almost everything Hitchens predicted about the war, vaunting his 'Twenty-Twenty Foresight', turned out to be conclusively, catastrophically wrong. For example: 'Will an Iraq war make our Al Qaeda problem worse? Not likely' – a point of view not even shared by the governments making war.[47] In the end the mounting threat to his credibility was so severe that the man who said, 'Ha ha ha, and yah, boo' to the antiwar movement, and serially slandered the likes of Cindy Sheehan and Naomi Klein, could not take 'the taunting' any more.[48]

But his more arresting response to the crisis of the occupation was to turn extraordinarily sanguinary. Following the November 2004 siege of Fallujah, Hitchens remarked that 'the death toll is not nearly high enough … too many [jihadists] have escaped'. That the insurgency arose primarily as an al-Qaeda–Ba'athist conspiracy, and not as an utterly predictable response to the occupation of Iraq, destruction of its infrastructure, murder of protesters, and empowerment of sectarian political forces, could thus serve to justify a quite shrill display of bloodlust. And when pressed, Hitchens did not hesitate to suggest that the Islamists should be wiped out:

> We can't live on the same planet as them and I'm glad because I don't want to. I don't want to breathe the same air as these psychopaths and murders [sic] and rapists and torturers and child abusers. It's them or me. I'm very happy about this because I know it will be them. It's a duty and a responsibility to defeat them. But it's also a pleasure. I don't regard it as a grim task at all.[49]

He later told those present at the christening of the David Horowitz Freedom Center that 'it's sort of a pleasure as well as a duty to kill these people.'[50] Years later, when Hitchens was speaking in Madison, Wisconsin, he was asked a question about Iran. His answer shocked even the conservatives in the audience: 'As for that benighted country, I wouldn't shed a tear if it was wiped off the face of this earth.'[51] That these barbaric vocables were uttered by someone ostensibly interested in the advancement of humanity, in solidarity and civilization, is by no means novel. It was a common response to the affront of anticolonial rebels, particularly those deemed under the influence of 'Mohammedan fanaticism'. As Dickens had put it, on hearing of the Indian rebellion of 1857 and reading the atrocity stories circulated in the British newspapers:

I would address that oriental character which must be powerfully spoken to, in something like the following placard ... 'I, the Inimitable, holding this office of mine ... have the honour to inform you Hindoo gentry that it is my intention, with all possible avoidance of unnecessary cruelty and with all merciful swiftness of execution, to exterminate the Race from the face of the earth, which disfigured the earth with abominable atrocities.[52]

In this respect also Hitchens was a highly typical, if not stereotypical, figure.

THE BOY WHO CRIED WOLF: GUILT BY ASSOCIATION

By the end of 2002 Hitchens was a signed-up member of the Committee for the Liberation of Iraq, a venture launched and headed by Bruce Jackson of the Project for the New American Century and formerly vice president of Lockheed Martin. Hitchens had been impressed by his earlier lunch meeting with Defense Secretary Donald Rumsfeld's subaltern, Paul Wolfowitz, who did his best to 'live down' his reputation as a neoconservative. For, the deputy defense secretary claimed, it was he who had persuaded the Reagan administration to dump its relationship with the Marcos dictatorship – 'the opposite of a Kissinger policy', he avowed, evidently running into another of Hitchens's psychic trip wires. In fact, the pair seemed to get on extremely well at their Pentagon lunch, as Hitchens explained to Ian Parker of the *New Yorker*.

'Wolfowitz was not asking my advice about Iraq, don't run away with that idea,' Hitchens said. 'He just felt that those who worked for the ousting of Saddam should get on closer terms with each other.' According to Wolfowitz's advisor Kevin Kellems, who attended the meeting, 'Hitchens said, "I was trying to signal you" through his writing, and Wolfowitz said, "I wondered."' Hitchens disputed that memory; he did remember asking Wolfowitz 'for reassurances that, in the event of an invasion, the United States would protect the Kurds from the Turks. They talked about Rwanda and Bosnia, about the history of genocide and the cost of inaction.' Kellems, who later became a friend of Hitchens's, described 'two giant minds unleashed in the room. They were finishing each other's sentences.' Hitchens described Wolfowitz as a 'bleeding heart', and he added, 'There are not many Republicans, or Democrats, who lie awake at night worrying about what's happening to the Palestinians, but he does.'[53]

Wolfowitz later assured Hitchens that, far from bolstering Sharon's war against the Palestinians, with the removal of an Arab rejectionist state the US would be in a position to demand the dismantling of settlements. And Hitchens praised Wolfowitz for 'tackling the racist assumption that Arabs preferred, or even needed, to be ruled by despots'.[54] If the thought occurred to Hitchens that the assumption that Arabs preferred, or even needed, to have their affairs decided by the American armed forces was just as racist, he did not express it. Whether by dint of Wolfowitz's guile or Hitchens's credulous predisposition, the serenade seems to have persuaded the writer. 'I was very flattered, I suppose, some might say I had been unduly impressed,' Hitchens admitted.[55]

At the very least, he persuaded himself 'that those within the administration who were making the case for "regime change" were sincere in what they believed and were not knowingly exaggerating anything for effect'. Likewise, during his time with the Pentagon and Wolfowitz, he

> never heard anything alarmist on the WMD issue. It was presumed that at some level Iraq remained a potential WMD state, and it was assumed that Saddam Hussein would never agree to come into compliance even with Hans Blix's very feeble 'inspections' (which indeed he never did).[56]

From that point on, it seems fair to say, Hitchens effectively made himself an amanuensis of the Bush administration, policing dissent, vituperating against its most effective opponents, lying about whatever, whomever. In much the same capacity he cried 'Wolf' whenever his friend and ally was criticised. Hitchens became a stolid advocate not only of Wolfowitz but of those, such as Ahmed Chalabi, whom the writer perceived as belonging to the factions of neo-Jeffersonians. Indeed, Chalabi and Wolfowitz had known each other since Richard Perle had introduced them in the 1980s, and Wolfowitz, along with Doug Feith, Donald Rumsfeld, and Dick Cheney, was integral to persuading Wolfowitz to support Chalabi as a potential ruler of 'the new Iraq'. So there was indeed a faction here, even if it placed Hitchens in some company he would have preferred to disavow. Indeed, he might have tended under pressure to forget all about the role of the secretary of defense and the vice president in lobbying for war. Taunted about his glorious Iraq war as it slid into catastrophe in 2006, he retorted that it was indeed glorious and 'it IS my war because it needed Paul Wolfowitz and myself to go and convince the President to go to war.'[57]

Against those who espied a sinister motive in the neoconservative drive to war with Iraq, Hitchens continued to heap praise on Paul

Wolfowitz, who he said had 'stressed the menace of Saddam Hussein since as far back as 1978' and had thus 'been right all along'. Hitchens was most likely referring to an analysis drafted for Wolfowitz while he was deputy assistant secretary of defense for regional programs, which was one of a number of similar analyses that sought to justify increased defence spending by urging preparation for what were deemed unlikely contingencies. Wolfowitz was thus only as right as the sexed-up intelligence; or as right as the neoconservative remilitarisation project; as right as he was about the Communist threat in South East Asia while he was Reagan's man in Indonesia, thoroughly imbricated with the Suharto dictatorship as it went about its murderous business in East Timor; or as right on this as he was about the Soviet threat in Nicaragua and El Salvador, which Hitchens knew was a pretext for US death squad diplomacy in both countries. Still, Wolfowitz was a 'bleeding heart' who should have his way on Iraq and, when it came to it, the presidency of the World Bank. Later, when Wolfowitz was caught redhanded, as it were, engaging in corruption (lobbying directly for a substantial pay increase and a promotion for his partner) as well as using his position to impose Bush administration policies such as the elimination of family planning programmes, Hitchens wasted no time in springing to the defence of Wolfowitz and his concomitant, Shaha Riza.[58]

Another making a claim on Hitchens's loyalty, at all costs to his probity, was Ahmed Chalabi. Hitchens would not hear a word said against this literate, cultured, humane democrat, whose forces, he claimed, 'provided invaluable help and intelligence' during the invasion and occupation of Iraq. (In fact, these forces, the Free Iraqi Forces militia, were a tiny, risible, poorly trained monument to Chalabi's narcissism.) It is understandable that Hitchens would be impressed by Chalabi, whose immense charm and energy had wooed others such as Labour MP Ann Clwyd. Moreover, Chalabi's nostalgia for the era before the Qassem revolt of 1958, when a monarchy under de facto British control assured what he argued was a real democracy, may have struck a chord with Hitchens.

Naturally, he denied the charge that Chalabi had fed false or misleading information to the US government to enable its drive to war. Hitchens's loyalty to Chalabi also permitted him to forgive sins of which he was typically less forgiving in others. For example, he could rationalise Chalabi's dabbling with sectarian politics (in effect, by saying that everyone else in Iraq is doing it) and his closeness to the Islamic Republic (Hitchens couldn't think of a better man to broker with Tehran). More pathetic was Hitchens's affected agnosticism at Chalabi's conviction, in absentia, by a Jordanian court for the embezzlement of $300 million:

> I do not know what happened at the Petra Bank, and not even Andrew and Patrick Cockburn, who have done the most work on the subject, can be sure that Saddam Hussein's agents in Jordan were not involved in the indictment of Chalabi by a rather oddly constituted Jordanian court. It could be, for all I know, that he was both guilty and framed. The litigation and recrimination continues, and it ought at least to be noted that Chalabi still maintains he can prove his case.[59]

Of course, it is true that Chalabi has always claimed that he was the victim of a stitch-up by agents of the Ba'athist dictatorship. It is also true that no one can be sure that he is wrong; indeed, it is hard to think of any piece of evidence that could disprove it. But if Ba'athist agents were involved, how would Chalabi know? And if he does know, he must also be able to explain how they engineered the collapse of the Chalabi family's Petra Bank interests in Geneva and Beirut and the string of criminal investigations that followed. He must also know how Saddam's finest spooks suborned Chalabi's ship-financing deal with the felon and brothel-owner Wayne Drizin and then induced it to collapse without anyone's knowing where the $15 million stake went. Similar deals with the Jordanian businessman Taj Hajjar and the Greek financier Spyridon Aspiotis led to arrests and charges, again presumably orchestrated by the Iraqi *mukhabarat*. Finally, these agents must have engineered the collapse of Jordan's financial system, the discovery of cooked books in Petra Bank, and Chalabi's abscondment before he even attempted to 'prove his case'. It would be good to know if a tithe of this is true.

Whatever one thinks of these charges, there is something more than disquieting about Hitchens's saying that his close friend Chalabi may well be a fraud and a liar – 'I do not know' – and in the same article affirming that he is the man to be Iraq's 'Mr Shiite'. This is not an abstract consideration. Iraq under occupation was a cesspit of financial corruption, fuelled by streams of money disbursed through the patrimonial, clientelist state built by the US. Chalabi's name almost always comes up when missing money in Iraq is discussed. He certainly benefitted directly when, as a member of the Interim Governing Council, he helped to install his son as the head of the Trade Bank of Iraq and his Card Tech company was subsequently awarded a contract by the same bank.[60] Not only that but Chalabi had played a role in building support for an invasion among Iraqi exiles, helping with the planning for a postwar Iraq, and supplying a stream of dubious intelligence sources to the Pentagon to help justify the war. If he was a fraudster, this might not be a propitious thing for Iraq. This does not seem to have given Hitchens any pause: here was Iraq's mahatma, and they should count themselves lucky to have him.

HOLLOW MAN: THE KILLING OF MARK DAILY

'I don't remember ever feeling, in every allowable sense of the word, quite so hollow.'[61] Hitchens had just confirmed that Lieutenant Mark Daily had gone to fight and die in Iraq, prompted to do so by a sample of the author's ludicrous chest beating. It is rare that such a direct connection is traceable between a writer's words and their consequences. But Hitchens *just felt awful*. Awful enough to compare himself with the poet Yeats:

> Over-dramatizing myself a bit in the angst of the moment, I found I was thinking of William Butler Yeats, who was chilled to discover that the Irish rebels of 1916 had gone to their deaths quoting his play *Cathleen ni Houlihan*. He tried to cope with the disturbing idea in his poem 'Man and the Echo':
>
> > Did that play of mine send out
> > Certain men the English shot? …
> > Could my spoken words have checked
> > That whereby a house lay wrecked?
>
> Abruptly dismissing any comparison between myself and one of the greatest poets of the 20th century …

Indeed, it perhaps is as well that, having raised it, Hitchens thought to dismiss the comparison. But things grew worse. Each new revelation compounded how much of Daily's foolish journey into Iraq had been inspired by choice words from the author.

> I feverishly clicked on all the links from the article and found myself on Lieutenant Daily's MySpace site, where his statement 'Why I Joined' was posted … And there, at the top of the page, was a link to a passage from one of my articles, in which I poured scorn on those who were neutral about the battle for Iraq.

It seemed that Daily had tried, according to his parents, to contact Hitchens.

> 'He thought maybe his e-mail had not reached you ...' That was a gash in my hide all right: I think of all the junk e-mail I read every day, and then reflect that his precious one never got to me.

And when it turned out that Daily had tried to get his hometown twinned with the Iraqi city of Dahok, 'I was wrenched yet again to discover that he had got this touching idea from an old article of mine, which had made a proposal for city-twinning that went nowhere.'

There seemed to be no getting away from the fact that Hitchens had helped at least one young man perish in a sickening blood orgy. But Hitchens was not about to forget his cues:

> If America can spontaneously produce young men like Mark, and occasions like this one, it has a real homeland security instead of a bureaucratic one. To borrow some words of George Orwell's when he first saw revolutionary Barcelona, 'I recognized it immediately as a state of affairs worth fighting for' ... Orwell thought that the Spanish Civil War was a just war, but he also came to understand that it was a dirty war, where a decent cause was hijacked by goons and thugs, and where betrayal and squalor negated the courage and sacrifice of those who fought on principle. As one who used to advocate strongly for the liberation of Iraq (perhaps more strongly than I knew), I have grown coarsened and sickened by the degeneration of the struggle: by the sordid news of corruption and brutality (Mark Daily told his father how dismayed he was by the failure of leadership at Abu Ghraib) and by the paltry politicians in Washington and Baghdad who squabble for precedence while lifeblood is spent and spilled by young people whose boots they are not fit to clean.[62]

This maudlin display of his grief and catharsis, in some ways even more stomach lurching than his tribute to the World Trade Center, thus climaxed in a puddle of self-pity and self-vindication. He had not supported the betrayal that the war on Iraq became. He had merely fantasised that the Bush administration was the equivalent of the Workers' Party of Marxist Unification, and he was *shocked* to find that they were selling out his just war. Yes, Hitchens felt awful – so awful that he shed his tears, took the occasion to vindicate himself once again, and then moved on without ever having to really account for what he had done.

CONCLUSION: TWENTY-TWENTY BLINDFOLD

I think it's a certainty that historians will not conclude that the removal of Saddam Hussein was something that the international community ought to have postponed any further.

– Christopher Hitchens, 'No Regrets'

HOW THINGS COULD HAVE BEEN

It is one thing to say that Hitchens was unable to get the war on terror right even in hindsight, despite the abundant evidence piling up like so much wreckage before Walter Benjamin's angel of history. A far more severe indictment is to say that his self-imposed blinds prevented him from understanding where real liberation in the Middle East would begin. For an ostensible – one might even say, ostentatious – internationalist of Hitchens's type, this is stern condemnation. Let me begin with hindsight.

It was not that Hitchens did not notice the smoking, carrion-filled craters perforating Iraq's major cities, the blitzed vehicles lining its motorways, the torture chambers (one business that did expand in the new Iraq), or the new mass graves. At least he could not completely deny the havoc that had been caused. He did, naturally, try to talk down the real level of destruction – for example, by characterising the *Lancet* survey into excess deaths in Iraq as 'politicised hack-work', a crazed fabrication whose conclusions had been 'conclusively and absolutely shown to be false'.[1] But even Hitchens's ingenuity had limits in such circumstances, so he adopted an alternative approach, insisting that everything could have worked out so beautifully, if only the Arab part of Iraq had been like the plucky Kurdish North:

Under the protective canopy of the no-fly zone – actually it was also called the 'you-fly-you-die zone' – an embryonic free Iraq had a chance to grow. I was among those who thought and believed and argued that this example could, and should, be extended to the rest of the country; the cause became a consuming thing in my life. To describe the resulting shambles as a disappointment or a failure or even a defeat would be the weakest statement I could possibly make: it feels more like a sick, choking nightmare of betrayal from which there can be no awakening. Yet Kurdistan continues to demonstrate how things could have been different, and it isn't a place from which the West can simply walk away.[2]

The Kurds had always been his moral sanction, the surety of his rectitude, the bulwark against disabling doubt. Who were a few peaceniks compared to a Kurdish resistance leader like Barham Saleh? What were 'riff-raff' like Muqtada al-Sadr compared to a freedom fighter like Jalal al-Talabani? Again, the integrity of his position was buttressed by sentiment.

The obvious difficulty with such a position was that northern Iraq's relative peace was possible only because there was a pro-US statelet already in place; no 'de-Ba'athification' would occur in northern Iraq, no destruction of the infrastructure, no 'Wolves Brigade' analogue, and no construction of a patrimonial state principally based on corruption and religious sectarianism.

True, the northern statelet had its repressive side, as when an Iraqi Kurd writer was jailed for thirty years for criticising the Kurdish regional leader Massoud Barzani.[3] But in this respect it was no more repressive than Turkey, the other regional state known to lock up Kurds for dissent.

Equally, the *peshmergas* (Kurdish freedom fighters) did not take long to act out the miserable logic according to which the organisations of oppressed people become agents of oppression once allied with imperialist power. Among the ethnic cleansers in a postwar Iraq were those trying to create a sort of 'Greater Kurdistan', one that would include as few Arabs as possible, and where the Assyrian Christian population would be halved.[4] But, again, the Kurdish statelet faced none of the most appallingly baleful conditions of occupation, and its leadership stood to gain from the situation (both in terms of land and national power); therefore the severity of the crisis and insurgency afflicting the majority of the country did not befall the Kurdish North.

Whichever way you look at it, Iraqi Kurdistan does not remotely demonstrate 'how things could have been different' in the rest of Iraq.

Yet it may be argued that the revolutions in Tunisia and Egypt demonstrate how things might have been different in Iraq without the Jeffersonian empire, and how quickly entrenched dictatorships can crumble – and with how much joyous unity among those responsible for their downfall. Hitchens admired the American state as a revolutionary, humanitarian force. But while the US seemed to perpetuate only repression, it was striking that the insurgents of 2011 produced Tahrir Square as their symbol of solidarity, resistance, and direct democracy. But they could not have produced an Abu Ghraib or a Fallujah, symbols of barbarism on a par with My Lai. Iraq was denied its Tahrir moment, which ought to have produced a moment of pause if Hitchens still had any of his old critical impulses. No such thought seemed to delay him. Worse, owing to the dictatorship's battle with the Islamist folk devil and its pro-Washington stance, he was for a time a public apologist for one of the dictatorships that fell to revolution.

'WHY PICK ON MILD TUNISIA?'

Before the Jasmine revolution in Tunisia, Hitchens's writing about this 'frontline territory between Europe and Africa' had been elegiac. His contrasts were Kiplingesque, and if 'the twain should have met' anywhere, it was surely here. Certainly, Tunisia had a dictatorship. But it had scored real accomplishments, deserving of celebration with great vim and gusto: its banning of the Islamist opposition, above all the group An-Nahda, and the exiling of its leader Rachid Ghannouchi, who was nonetheless 'allowed to broadcast his hysterical incitements into Tunisia from a London station'. Moreover, 'people do not lower their voices or look over their shoulders … before discussing these questions'.[5] If this was a dictatorship, it was decidedly Europeanised; it was not fully African, at any rate. And so he told *Vanity Fair* readers:

> Why pick on mild Tunisia, where the coup in 1987 had been bloodless, where religious parties are forbidden, where the population grows evenly because of the availability of contraception, where you can see male and female students holding hands and wearing blue jeans, and where thousands of Americans and more than four million Europeans take their vacations every year?[6]

When the 2010–11 uprising began, the era opened by 2001 was drawn abruptly to a close. The revolt and the coterminous protest movements in neighbouring states demanded a new schema and a new political language for interpreting events. The masses, so long excluded from Arab history by a chain of dictators, most of them in the US fold, had asserted themselves – not as fodder for counterinsurgency or intervention but as agents of their own destiny. Hitchens declined any opportunity to learn a new language.

Rather than reflect on whether the Tunisian success story that he had regurgitated for *Vanity Fair* in 2007 was perhaps a bit overdone, he proceeded as if he had been confirmed in his analysis. Tunisia was the 'most civilized dictatorship' in the Middle East, he insisted, whose subjects rebelled because 'they knew they could. There was scant likelihood of the sort of all-out repression and bloodshed that was met by, say, the protesters against the Iranian mullahs.'[7] This was untrue: the death toll from the Tunisian revolution stood at 224 by its end. The death toll from the suppression of the Iranian Green movement was 72, according to the opposition.[8] But, more to the point, it was a preposterously reactionary thing to say. We are well used to politicians in liberal democracies offering stern lectures to protesters to the effect that their mere ability to protest demonstrates the relatively benign nature of the social order they protest against. This is silliness on stilts. But to say such a thing about a dictatorship when its victims were still warm was a Blimpism worthy of the latter-day Conor Cruise O'Brien.

Tunisia's revolution deserves a better explanation than this. For it seemed that while Hitchens was enjoying the relaxed atmosphere of Tunisian cafes and chatting up friendly academics, a powerful dynamic simply passed him by. The Ben Ali regime, like all the region's dictatorships, had experienced a dramatic narrowing of its social base as a result of the neoliberal policies it had imposed with the connivance of the International Monetary Fund. In most cases this involved weakened trade unions, the privatisation of public goods, deregulation, and cuts to social security programmes, with the effect of enriching an ever-narrower elite and disenfranchising sections of the population that had previously been relatively secure.

The dictator Ben Ali was primarily responsible for introducing such policies into Tunisia. Despite his pledge to democratise the country, he reinforced these policies with increased repression. Combining rigged elections and interference in the country's trade union federation (which had long been a partner of the ruling party, going back to their cooperation in the anticolonial movement) with torture and the use of military courts, Ben Ali took out one opposition force after another – the trade union left, the Communists, and the Islamists. As the regime's base of support became ever more slender, the internal security apparatus was expanded. The final decomposition of the regime resulted from three weak points: the continued existence of a trade union movement that, though wholly co-opted, had latent power that was unleashed during the revolt; the desire of the army to hold to its constitutional role and avoid direct involvement in repression; and the existence of elite factions that were not wholly integrated into the regime and could thus break from it.[9]

Hitchens had, as I have shown, broken with any critique of capitalism even in its neoliberal form. Free markets and free people went together. As such he had no basis for understanding what was really going on in Tunisian society. And for all that he cautiously welcomed the revolt when it happened, he shuddered at the emergence of An-Nahda leaders from exile to participate in the new democracy. 'Better the bullet than the ballot box', seemed to be Hitchens's motto when dealing with the Islamists.

Hitchens' evasions and revisions on Tunisia segued neatly into his pouring cold water on the Egyptian revolution, which he suggested (writing in early February) would likely fail, as 'the Arab world is almost completely unlettered and unversed' in 'the language of civil society'.[10] Hitchens was not lacking in sympathy for the revolutionaries. He took heart from the absence of mass Islamist movements' rushing to take power, saluting the 'really admirable solidity and maturity, both in their civic conduct and in their demands' of the revolutionaries.[11] But he asserted that Egypt lacked 'a genuine opposition leader' and its political parties, with the exception of the Muslim Brotherhood, were 'emaciated hulks'. This account was exaggerated and unfairly condescending. Egyptian civil society had been developing and maturing under the despot's integument during the preceding decade, beginning with pro-Palestine and antiwar activism, building to a remarkably broad coalition of liberals, socialists, and Islamists by 2005. There followed the first eruptions of an organised and independent labour movement whose strikes inspired the 'April 26' movement. This coalition, with the labour movement proving important in the later stages, broke the Mubarak dictatorship and its backers. Egyptians were not, after all, so unlettered and unversed in the language of civil society.

In addition to being condescending, Hitchens's argument was hypocritical. For, despite his symptomatic reticence about the meaning of the revolutions underway, despite his caution about their potential outcome, he was all too happy to attempt, feebly, to use them to cast some retrospective logic on the invasion of Iraq. The 'Iraq effect', he claimed, should be credited for these revolutions. And in a sense he was right: a key stage in the development of the revolution had been the incubation of much of its activist core in the fight against that war. But, although he was discussing regimes in which the major bulwark of external support had been the US, he wagered that the real counterrevolutionary force, absent the occupation of Iraq, would have been Saddam Hussein. (Of course, Hussein would still be in power: Arabs were capable of overthrowing a well-entrenched dictatorship backed by the world's most powerful military state, this reasoning went, but were not capable of overthrowing an enfeebled dictatorship encircled by the world's powers.) Thus the invasion had been 'an unnoticed and unacknowledged benefit whose extent is impossible to compute'.[12]

The fault line in Hitchens's politics, in both cases, was his hatred for the Islamists and, at bottom, his bigoted attitude towards Muslims. Such attitudes had expressed themselves in an exchange, recorded by an unusually sycophantic journalist in 2005, between Hitchens and a number of Iraqi exiles. Though supportive of Bush's occupation, these Iraqis were offended by Hitchens's colonial sensibilities:

> Christopher Hitchens said to Ghassan Atiyyah: 'If the Iraqis were to elect either a Sunni or Shia Taliban, we would not let them take power' …
>
> But Atiyyah would have none of that. He exploded in furious rage. 'So you're my colonial master now, eh?!' You have to understand – this man's voice really carries.
>
> Suddenly, Atiyyah did have defenders at the table. I could see that coming in the shocked expressions on the faces of the other Iraqis when they heard what Hitchens said.[13]

Hitchens, whatever he thought of democracy, seems to have distrusted the peoples of the Middle East with such a precious gift, because of the strong likelihood at this conjuncture that many millions would choose to vote for Islamist parties in rejection of the old dictatorships and of US domination. So, if they were to experiment with self-government, better they should do so under American military supervision and guard. And, if this earned the US 'the hate of those ye guard', that was just bad luck.

By February 2011 Libya had joined the list of dictatorships then under the protective canopy of the US and that had started to undergo revolution. One might think that at this stage, Hitchens would have finally learned his lesson. No such thing. Libya's revolution was also decisively

the product of the invasion of Iraq: a 'British diplomat who helped nego-
tiate the surrender of Qaddafi's stockpile of WMD' confirmed as much.
'Qaddafi's abject fear at watching the fate of Saddam Hussein' ensured
his acquiescence, thus depriving him of the sorts of weapons he might
have deployed against the revolution. True, he 'remained a filthy nuisance', as he 'forced Western oil companies to pay the $1.5 billion fine
levied on him for Lockerbie', but he was less of a nuisance because of
American intimidation.[14]

The major trouble with this line is that Gadhafi had been attempting to make peace with both the European Union and the US since the
1990s, on the prosaic ground that he hoped to get sanctions lifted. The
second problem is that Gadhafi's weapons of mass destruction were, in
a sense, hypothetical. The centrepiece of his 'stockpile of WMD' was a
nuclear weapons programme. Lacking serious funding of the sort that
the USSR might once have been able to provide, the programme had
advanced to the embryonic stage by 2004, with a few elements such
as yellow cake, centrifuges, and so on. But no actual weapon had been
achieved, far less a stockpile. And suffice to say, centrifuges are of little
use in battle with revolutionaries. Furthermore, the movement toward
abandoning the programme had been initiated in the late 1990s as an
aspect of Gadhafi's attempt to come in from the cold, and its culmination was *delayed* rather than hastened by the Bush administration's
aggressive policy. To undo the damage required a climb down from this
bellicosity, and an offer to incorporate Gadhafi under the US umbrella
in consideration of a very public disarmament.[15]

Still, if Hitchens struggled to keep the narrative straight, and took
pains not to notice that the US, and particularly his neoconservative
allies, had been embedded with the Gadhafi regime since 2004, he
nonetheless embraced this revolution, seemingly without any of the
telltale hesitation or reticence about its politics. The question, given his
previous indications, is why?

WHY PICK ON LIBYA?

In principle there was much for Hitchens to like about Gadhafi's regime.
Here was a society where religious parties were banned. True, this is
because *all* opposition parties were banned, but this gave Hitchens only
the slightest pause in Tunisia. More than this, it was a regime that exter-
minated the Islamist opposition and had done so since well before the
war on terror. It was also a regime that had come to power as a result
of a bloodless coup, just as had Ben Ali. It was a state where women

had more freedom than in many neighbouring states. And its leadership was directly allied with that of the United States. What more could he desire? Perhaps Hitchens was simply ignorant about Libya, a conclusion strongly indicated by his remarks on its WMD stockpiles.[16] But this would not necessarily have decided the matter. Of course, Hitchens would never have simply and unambiguously embraced dictatorship. However corrupted and contradictory his moral stances had become by 2011, a straightforward defence of tyranny would have been beyond the pale for him. Yet, whereas with Tunisia, and to a lesser extent Egypt, he was hesitant and even slightly grudging in his support for the revolutions, there was never a moment's doubt with Libya.

I will advance a number of simple explanations here. The first is that on some indexes Gadhafi's regime was worse than the others, particularly in its inability to allow any form of organised opposition, even a tame loyal opposition, in the Jamahiriya. The second is that it had been in conflict with the US for longer than it had been in alliance with it, and there was every chance that Gadhafi could be dispensed with – as indeed he was in the end. Most important, from Hitchens's perspective, the Libyan revolution seemed to present an opportunity to restore the prestige of American military power.

As soon as it became clear that the Libyan revolutionaries were potentially facing defeat, and that their political leadership might be open to an alliance with NATO, Hitchens rounded on the Obama White House for having dithered over Tunisia and Egypt. Would it now do nothing while Gadhafi, 'an all-round stinking nuisance and moreover a long-term *enemy*', hunted down the opposition? Railing against the cautious realpolitikers in the White House, he insisted:

> In the Mediterranean, the United States maintains its Sixth Fleet, which could ground Qaddafi's air force without breaking a sweat … The United States, with or without allies, has unchallengeable power in the air and on the adjacent waters. It can produce great air lifts and sea lifts of humanitarian and medical aid, which will soon be needed anyway along the Egyptian and Tunisian borders, and which would purchase undreamed-of goodwill. It has the chance to make up for its pointless, discredited tardiness with respect to events in Cairo and Tunis.[17]

The war was an opportunity to once again moralise the means of violence at America's disposal. This had long been a concern of Hitchens's. Evidently looking for this moment, for the next righteous conflict, he thought he had spied it in Iran, after the Green movement kicked off in 2009. Unsurprisingly, in addition to crediting the Tunisian, Egyptian, and Libyan revolutions to the invasion of Iraq, he also fancied that the green movement was 'partly created by the invasion of Iraq'. And so it would only be fitting for the US to finish the job by invading Iran. And if the Iranian people did not request that kind of help?

> We can simply say, 'We're not going to stay. We're handing the country over to you. We're not occupying. We don't want to stay. We can't wait to get out. And you've been de-Revolutionary-Guardized. Cry all you want.'
>
> We will have done them a favor, and ourselves. We have rights, too. The international community has rights. The U.N. has rights. The U.S. has rights. The IAEA [International Atomic Energy Agency] has rights. The Iranians made deals with all of them, and they broke them.[18]

That Hitchens's profoundly colonial contempt for the Iranians would tend to undermine any claim he would make to being an internationalist and democrat was presumably as lost on him as the irony of a promise from the US military, in 2010, not to overstay its welcome.

But the same predisposition was evident when he turned his attention to Libya. For there too it was not of primary importance whether Libyans actually wanted an intervention. Acknowledging in early March that the revolutionaries still appeared 'to want this achievement [the overthrow of Gadhafi] to represent their own unaided effort', Hitchens insisted that 'it doesn't excuse us from responsibility'. This was because Gadhafi's revolutionary foreign policy was a security menace. 'Even if Gadhafi basked in the unanimous adoration of his people, he would not be entitled to the export of violence,' Hitchens observed. Accepting that he was indeed scandalised by the 'export of violence', it is odd that he chose to cite policies long since abandoned, dropped when the Gadhafi regime began making eyes at the US.

As ever, Hitchens's position contained an element of narcissism: 'I am sure I am not alone in feeling rather queasy about being forced to watch the fires in Tripoli and Benghazi as if I were an impotent spectator.'[19] America should act so that Hitchens would not feel impotent: the US military as a lethal phallic substitute.

TERMINUS

The logical nadir of Hitchens's nationalist identification with the American state was his propensity to fetishise its most repressive and aggressive apparatus, the military. Hitchens could not stand the petty bureaucracy of being searched at an airport, but a bureaucrat with a rifle and insignia was sacred. The military could redeem any situation, and nowhere was its presence questionable. Moreover, no matter the situation, no matter the emergency, the US Army was always picking up fantastic experience in the frontiers that would be of immense use in the near future:

> It's very important we find out and get better at response to failed state and rogue state combinations, because we're going to be doing this again … There's a lot to go wrong in Syria, a great deal to go wrong in Iran, which is found to be cheating with its nukes and is run by the theocracy that has pushed the country into the ground. The ground we're gaining in Iraq, and one reason I support the war, is that the U.S. army is learning fantastically useful lessons in how to do this, as well as rebuilding.[20]

However, these lessons were not just for use overseas. Amid the utter devastation of Katrina, for example, after some duration in which US government officials had withheld aid and obstructed relief agencies, the armed forces were eventually deployed. The *Army Times* referred to the victims of this horror as 'the insurgency'. Brigadier General Gary Jones, who headed the Louisiana National Guard's Joint Task Force, had promised a 'combat operation' to 'take this city back' – even if it would turn the place into a 'Little Somalia' in the process. So it is instructive that, when Hitchens was challenged about the Bush administration's conduct, he retorted that the problem was that the governor of Louisiana had not asked for the president to send the troops in early enough. In a piece of rhetorical bravado – or a lie, as it might less politely be called – Hitchens went on to claim that the troops had 'learned in Iraq matters of civil reconstruction, water distribution, purification, that have been extremely useful to them in New Orleans'.[21] Naturally, every word of this was nonsense: the Army Corps of Engineers needed no tour of Iraq, its infrastructure devastated many times over by the occupation, to learn its trade. But the miracles of empire were endless.

When, after a year of global recession, and his own *manque à gagner*, Hitchens wrote a diatribe for *Vanity Fair* complaining about the dereliction of the US infrastructure, the incompetence and corruption of the US polity, the depredations of bankers and the 'moneyed class', he remembered to acquit the army on all counts and even to pay it this lavish tribute in the concluding paragraph:

In banana republics, admittedly, very often the only efficient behavior is displayed by the army (and the secret police). But our case is rather different. In addition to exhibiting extraordinary efficiency and, most especially under the generalship of David Petraeus, performing some great feats of arms and ingenuity, the American armed forces manifest all the professionalism and integrity that our rulers and oligarchs lack. Who was it who the stricken inhabitants of New Orleans and later of the Texas coastline yearned to see? Who was it who informed the blithering and dithering idiots at FEMA that they could have as many troops as they could remember to ask for, even as volunteers were embarking for Afghanistan and Iraq? What is one of the main engines of integration for blacks and immigrants, as well as one of the finest providers of education and training for those whom the system had previously failed? It may be true that the government has succeeded in degrading our armed forces as well – tasking them with absurdities and atrocities like Guantánamo and Abu Ghraib – but this only makes the banana-republic point in an even more emphatic way.[22]

This passage superficially resembles an argument. Yet for a conclusion it is decidedly inconclusive. It seems to be going somewhere with its argument about the role of the military in American society but stops short of any exhortation or recommendation. Implicitly, it seems to say: things would be perfectly swell if the military just ran everything, instead of these grasping parasites and crooked politicians. But that remains, at most, a disavowed subtext. And because the passage does not quite reach the level of an argument, it can only be treated finally as sentiment – sentiment reflecting an attitude of the most prostrate, boot-licking servility and devotion.

In Hitchens the reactionary and the progressive had always vied; the provincial from a military town had always competed with the cosmopolitan and internationalist, and so had the ironist with the red-faced literalist, the charming wit with the lumpen sadistic boor, the seditious with the servile.

The way in which he decided between these contrasts was settled in part by his sense of the wider historical trends, as well as the parochial trends favouring his own advance. If he tended to resolve these contradictions in favour of world revolution in his early adulthood, it was in part because there was a real historical process that he could identify as a dynamic force: he would be on the right side of history, even if he was only distributing the newspaper of a small Trotskyist organisation. However, as he did once say, misquoting Victor Hugo, 'The logic of history is pitiless.' The defeat of 1968 destroyed any faith he had in revolution. The decadence of social democracy left him with no faith in reformism. He was left with no sense of advance other than his personal escape from the poky confines of a decaying, damp England and into the American magazine circuit. The fall of the USSR and the absence of a resurgence of the workers' movement depleted whatever faith he had in socialism.

Finally, he had no sense of any dynamic historical force other than capitalism itself, the US as its major global advocate and defender, and the Islamist demon as its nemesis. He found, as he might have suspected, that being on the right side of history in this sense was to gain more influence and pecuniary advantage than ever before. He succumbed to *almost* every craven, supine, and bigoted impulse he possessed and, while despatching the false gods of other believers, adopted a devotional attitude towards his adopted land. He became 'a living and ignominious satire on himself'.

ACKNOWLEDGMENTS

Thanks are due to many people who were quick and generous with their help. This is not a biography, but in assessing Hitchens's life as a political writer, I have had to draw on the recall of his old friends and contacts. Among those who knew Christopher Hitchens, Tariq Ali, Alex Callinicos, D. D. Guttenplan, Sam Husseini, Stephen Marks, John Palmer, Dennis Perrin, John Rose, Michael Rosen, and Martin Tomkinson were all extremely generous with their time and memory.

John Helmer provided not only background, but also suggested many important contacts and leads. I also appreciate the willingness of Duncan Campbell, John Judis and Thomas Mallon to help.

Mark Pavlick provided considerable assistance, forwarding references and materials which I would not have otherwise seen, and putting me in touch with people I would not have thought to contact. I am also grateful to Ian Birchall, Fred Branfman and Noam Chomsky for their thoughtful replies to my queries.

I have also made use of interview material accumulated while writing *The Liberal Defence of Murder*. This includes conversations with the sadly late Marxists Chris Harman and Alexander Cockburn, but also with Sasha Abramsky, Alex Callinicos, Mike Davis, and Adam Shatz, and I should like to thank them again.

And I'd finally like to thank Rowan Wilson, Mark Martin and Sebastian Budgen at Verso for their patient assistance.

NOTES

PROLOGUE

1   *BBC News*, 'Christopher Hitchens Dies at 62 after Suffering Cancer', 16 December 2011.

2   Mark Fisher, *Capitalist Realism: Is There No Alternative?* Ropley: O Books, 2009.

3   Terry Eagleton, Review of *Hitch-22: A Memoir*, *New Statesman*, 31 May 2010.

4   Decca Aitkenhead, 'Christopher Hitchens: "I Was Right and They Were Wrong"', *Guardian* (London), 22 May 2010.

5   Edward W. Lempinen, 'How the Left Became Irrelevant', *Salon*, 29 October 2002.

6   MacIntyre was a member of the International Socialists for a period before Hitchens joined. A collection of MacIntyre's writings from this era can be found in Paul Blackledge and Neil Davidson, eds., *Alasdair MacIntyre's Engagement with Marxism: Selected Writings, 1953–1974*, Chicago: Haymarket Books, 2006.

7   Alasdair MacIntyre, 'Notes from the Moral Wilderness', in Blackledge and Davidson, *Alasdair MacIntyre's Engagement with Marxism*.

8   Tariq Ali, interview by author, 3 January 2012; James Fenton, 'Why Hitchens Became an American', *Slate*, 16 December 2011.

9   Adam Shatz, interview by author, originally published in Richard Seymour, *The Liberal Defence of Murder*, London: Verso, 2008, 241.

10 Ted Honderich, *Conservatism: Burke, Nozick, Bush, Blair?* London: Pluto, 2005; Corey Robin, *The Reactionary Mind: Conservatism from Edmund Burke to Sarah Palin*, Oxford: Oxford University Press, 2011; Corey Robin, 'Conservatives', unpublished essay. See also Corey Robin, 'Out of Place', *Nation*, 4 June 2008.

11 Christopher Hitchens, 'Regime Change', in *A Long Short War: The Postponed Liberation of Iraq*, New York: Plume, 2003, 53

12 Christopher Hitchens, 'Regime Change', in *A Long Short War: The Postponed Liberation of Iraq*, New York: Plume, 2003, 48. On the terminology as used in the Trotskyist tradition from which Hitchens graduated, see Chris Harman, *Bureaucracy and Revolution in Eastern Europe*, London: Pluto Press, 1974.

13 Christopher Hitchens, 'Imperialism', in *A Long Short War*, 32–3.

14 On the emergence and lineage of this discourse, see Nicolas Guilhot, *The Democracy Makers: Human Rights and International Order*, New York: Columbia University Press, 2005.

15 See Erez Manela, *The Wilsonian Moment: Self-Determination and the International Origins of Anticolonial Nationalism*, Oxford: Oxford University Press, 2007.

16 See 'Christopher Hitchens: Be Prepared to Lose a Town a Week!', YouTube, 15 July 2007.

17 Seymour, *Liberal Defence of Murder*, 21–2; Michael Ledeen, *Freedom Betrayed: How America Led a Global Democratic Revolution, Won the Cold War, and Walked Away*, Washington, DC: American Enterprise Institute, 1996.

18 Christopher Hitchens, *Hitch-22: A Memoir*, Atlantic Books, London, 2011, photoplate caption.

19 Christopher Hitchens, 'Hugo Boss', *Slate*, 2 August 2010.

20 Christopher Hitchens, *Hitch-22: A Memoir*, London: Allen & Unwin, 2011.

21 *Fox News*, 20 September 2006.

22 *ABC Lateline*, 26 February 2004. On the coup in Haiti see Peter Hallward, *Damming the Flood: Haiti, Aristide, and the Politics of Containment*, London: Verso, 2007.

23 On Hervé see Michael B. Loughlin, *The Political Transformation of Gustave Hervé: 1871–1944*, Bloomington: Indiana University Press, 1987. On Mussolini see Paul O'Brien, *Mussolini in the First World War: The Journalist, the Soldier, the Fascist*, Oxford: Berg, 2004. On Spargo see Markuu Ruotsila, *John Spargo and American Socialism*, London: Palgrave Macmillan, 2006, and Richard Seymour, 'John Spargo and American Socialism', *Historical Materialism* 17: 2, 2009.

24 David Edgar, 'With Friends Like These …', *Guardian*, 19 April 2008; Andrew Brown, 'Scourge and Poet', *Guardian*, 15 February 2003.

25 A good critique of this ideology of evil is provided by Corey Robin, *Fear: The History of a Political Idea*, Oxford: Oxford University Press, 2004. See also

Christopher Hitchens, 'Against Sinister Perfectionism', in *Unacknowledged Legislation: Writers in the Public Sphere*, London: Verso, 2002.

26 Isaac Deutscher, 'The Conscience of the Ex-Communist', review of *The God That Failed*, in the *Reporter*, April 1950. See Christopher Hitchens, 'Third Thoughts', in *For the Sake of Argument: Essays and Minority Reports*, London: Verso, 1993.

27 This comparison is suggested by John O'Sullivan, 'Hitch Observed', *National Review Online*, 20 February 2012. For examples of Hitchens's rudeness see Martin Amis, foreword to Windsor Mann, ed., *The Quotable Christopher Hitchens: From Alcohol to Zionism*, Boston: Da Capo Press, 2011.

28 See the devastating review by John Barrell, 'The Positions He Takes', *London Review of Books*, 30 November 2006.

29 See Christopher Hitchens, 'In Defence of Plagiarism', in *Unacknowledged Legislation*; O'Sullivan, 'Hitch Observed'.

30 Here, for example, is what Hitchens wrote in *The Trial of Henry Kissinger* about Operation Speedy Express, an assault on the civilian population of South Vietnam. Here Hitchens discusses the intelligence available to US officials regarding the presence of North Vietnamese units in an area that came under US attack: 'On 22 January 1968, Defense Secretary Robert McNamara had told the Senate that "no regular North Vietnamese units" were deployed in the Mekong Delta' (31). 'As late as January 22nd, 1968, Defense Secretary McNamara had testified before the Senate that "no regular North Vietnamese units" were engaged in the Delta.' Noam Chomsky and Edward S. Herman, *The Political Economy of Human Rights: Vol. 1: The Washington Connection and Third World Fascism*, Boston: South End Press, 1979, (313).

In *The Trial of Henry Kissinger* Hitchens goes on to quote several passages from a *Newsweek* report by Kevin Buckley describing overwhelming evidence of a US war against civilians. These are remarkably similar to those passages from Buckley cited by Chomsky and Herman in *The Political Economy of Human Rights*, before discussing some information kept in unpublished notes by Buckley: 'Other notes by Buckley … discovered the same telltale evidence in hospital statistics. In March 1969, the hospital at Ben Tre reported 343 patients injured by "friendly fire" and 25 by "the enemy" … And Buckley's own citation for his magazine – of "perhaps as many as 5,000 deaths" among civilians in this one sweep – is an almost deliberate understatement of what he was told by a United States official, who actually said that "at least 5,000" of the dead "were what we refer to as noncombatants"' (31–3).

And here are Chomsky and Herman, in 1979: 'Buckley's notes add further detail. In the single month of March, the Ben Tre hospital reported 343 people wounded by "friendly" fire as compared with 25 by "the enemy" … Buckley's actual citation about the "perhaps as many as 5,000 deaths" is to a senior pacification official who estimated "at least 5,000" of those killed "were what we refer to as non-combatants" ' (313–16).

Now, the intriguing thing about the similarity in these passages is that they even are identical in their slight misquotation of Buckley. Buckley's actual statement was that 'a staggering number of noncombatant civilians – perhaps as many as 5,000 according to one official – were killed by U.S. firepower'. More than that, these passages are similar in citing unpublished notes that Buckley gave to Chomsky and Herman, and both cite the same details from those notes in similar phrasing.

31 Tariq Ali, interview.

32 In fairness, Hitchens credited Sam Husseini's work in the chapter on health care in the paperback edition of *No One Left to Lie To*. But Hitchens's arguments about Operation Desert Fox were, seemingly by his own admission, also appropriated without credit. More routine forms of borrowing included the casual lifting of one-liners. Sam Husseini, interview by author, 25 May 2012; 'Resurrecting Christopher Hitchens', blog entry by Sam Husseini, 21 December 2011, husseini.posterous.com; Alexander Cockburn, 'Breasts, Martinis and Hitchens', *Counterpunch*, 6 May 2003.

33 Hitchens, 'In Defence of Plagiarism'. In fact, to be absolutely clear, Hitchens's defence concluded with a warning to readers and critics not to be too eager to spot plagiarism. I invite the reader to draw the obvious conclusion.

34 Two of the authors whom I contacted on this subject were perfectly happy with the way Hitchens used their material, as it would help get the facts to a wider audience.

35 See chapter 1 for the story of Hitchens's rapprochement with the 'ratbags'.

36 Alexander Cockburn, 'Hitch the Snitch', *Counterpunch*, 15 June 1999. John B. Judis, a former colleague of Hitchens's, recalled that in 1989, 'Hitchens showed me a column in which he had criticized Norman Podhoretz for comparing Gorbachev to Hitler. I was writing an essay on conservatives and decided to include this item because it perfectly illustrated the unwillingness of some conservatives to come to terms with the end of the cold war. Just to make sure, I called Hitchens to confirm that he had accurately characterized Podhoretz's words. He convinced me that this account was accurate, but, after the essay was published, I received an angry letter from Podhoretz, who enclosed the original column that he had written, which, I discovered, Hitchens had indeed mischaracterized. I published a retraction and an apology.' John B. Judis, 'Sid the Unvicious', *New Republic*, 8 March 1999.

1 CHRISTOPHER HITCHENS IN THEORY AND PRACTICE

1   'When I was a Marxist, I did not hold my opinions as a matter of faith but I did have the conviction that a sort of unified field theory might have been discovered. The concept of historical and dialectical materialism was not an absolute and it did not have any supernatural element, but it did have its messianic element in the idea that an ultimate moment might arrive, and it most certainly had its martyrs and saints and doctrinaires and (after a while) its mutually excommunicating rival papacies. It also had its schisms and inquisitions and heresy hunts.' Christopher Hitchens, *God Is Not Great: How Religion Poisons Everything*, New York: Random House, 2007. Kindle location 2218–21.

2   This point is well made by Terry Eagleton in *Reason, Faith and Revolution: Reflections on the God Debate*, New Haven, CT: Yale University Press, 2009, 124–7. On the same theme see Dan Hind, *The Threat to Reason: How the Enlightenment Was Hijacked and How We Can Reclaim It*, London: Verso, 2007, 63–5.

3   'A Discussion about Christopher Hitchens', *Charlie Rose*, 13 April 2012, charlierose.com.

4   D. D. Guttenplan, 'Changing Places', *Nation*, 28 July 2010.

5   Christopher Hitchens, 'On Not Knowing the Half of It: Homage to Telegraphist Jacobs', in *Prepared for the Worst: Selected Essays and Minority Reports*, London: Chatto & Windus, 1989.

6   Christopher Hitchens, *Hitch-22: A Memoir*, London: Allen & Unwin 2011.

7   Ibid., 771–83.

8   Ibid., 1167–70.

9   Ibid., 869; Decca Aitkenhead, 'Christopher Hitchens: "I Was Right and They Were Wrong" ', *Guardian* (London), 22 May 2010.

10   Alex Callinicos, interview by author, 17 July 2012.

11   John Palmer, interview by author, 12 May 2012; John Rose, interview by author, 13 May 2012; Stephen Marks, interview by author, 14 May 2012; Alex Callinicos, interview by author, 17 July 2012.

12   Rose, interview; Hitchens, *Hitch-22*, Kindle location 3252.

13   It may just as well be that Hitchens did not identify this as a particularly important aspect of his time in the International Socialists. Alex Callinicos recalls that the issue didn't really arise during his time as a member, although it did arise afterward.

14   Hitchens, *Hitch-22*, Kindle location 1632–33; Michael Rosen, interview by author, 3 May 2012. I am grateful to Michael Rosen for sharing with me the relevant email exchanges between him and Hitchens's publisher.

15   See Hitchens, *Hitch-22: A Memoir*, London: Atlantic Books, 2011, 83–4.

16 Christopher Hitchens, *Hitch-22: A Memoir*, Kindle locations 3937 and 3952, Allen & Unwin.

17 Harman added: 'I recall myself and John Rose bumping into him in a pub and him being visibly embarrassed by our presence.' Chris Harman, interview by author, 16 October 2006.

18 Alex Callinicos, interview by author, 17 July 2012.

19 For an illuminating, concise account of those remarkable days, see Peter Robinson, 'Portugal 1974–75: Popular Power', in Colin Barker, ed., *Revolutionary Rehearsals*, Chicago: Haymarket, 1987.

20 Callinicos suggests that Hitchens's critique may have been influenced by the position of the US Socialist Workers' Party, of which his then girlfriend was a member.

21 Christopher Hitchens, 'In the bright autumn of my senescence', *London Review of Books*, 16:1, 6 January 1994.

22 Rose, interview. Callinicos explains that this lapse was during a period in which the editors had attempted to give the paper a more populist, tabloidy feel, partly in an attempt to relate to youth currents such as the punk movement. The result was a decline in the usual ideological filters.

23 This may have been in part to advance his career, as a job interview with the *Times* of London had culminated in a query from his interviewer about whether Hitchens would be allowed to join it. The implication appeared to be that it would be more respectable to be that sort of a socialist than to be seen as a 'fellow traveller' of the far left. Hitchens, *Hitch-22*, Kindle location 2586.

24 Ibid., 3281–85; Rhys Southan, 'Free Radical', *Reason*, 1 November 2001.

25 Hitchens, *Hitch-22*, Kindle location 1648.

26 Christopher Hitchens, 'Iraq Flexes Arab Muscle', *New Statesman*, 2 April 1976, republished in *New Statesman*, 5 July 2007, newstatesman.com.

27 D. D. Guttenplan, interview by author, 10 May 2010; Richard Seymour, *The Liberal Defence of Murder*, London: Verso, 2008, 240.

28 Guttenplan, interview.

29 Hitchens, 'On Not Knowing the Half of It'; Lesley Hazleton, 'Hazleton on Hitchens', *Accidental Theologist*, 3 February 2012.

30 Hitchens, *Hitch-22*, Kindle location 7364–65.

31 See Edward Said, *Orientalism*, London: Penguin Books, 2003.

32 Guttenplan, interview.

33 Tariq Ali, interview by author, 3 January 2012.

34 Dennis Perrin, interview by author, 6 May 2012. On this issue see also Alexander Cockburn, 'Hitchens Backs Down: Says Sheehan "Not a LaRouchie"', *Counterpunch*, 24 August 2005.

35 See Richard J. Evans, *Telling Lies for Hitler: The Holocaust, History and the David Irving Trial*, London: Verso, 2002.

36 Christopher Hitchens, 'Critic of the Booboisie', in *Unacknowledged Legislation: Writers in the Public Sphere*, London: Verso, 2002, 167.

37 See Christopher Hitchens, 'The Strange Case of David Irving', in *Love, Poverty, and War: Journeys and Essays*, London: Atlantic Books, 2005.

38 Quoted, Martin Amis, foreword to Windsor Mann, *The Quotable Hitchens: From Alcohol to Zionism, The Very Best of Christopher Hitchens*, Philadelphia: Perseus Books, 2011, xiii.

39 Guttenplan, interview.

40 Ali, interview by author, 11 January 2012.

41 Guttenplan, interview.

42 Christopher Hitchens, 'The Clemency of Clinton', 'Clinton as a Rhodesian', and 'Bill's Bills in Miami', in *For the Sake of Argument: Essays and Minority Reports*, London: Verso, 1993.

43 See Christopher Hitchens, *No One Left to Lie To: The Values of the Worst Family*, London: Verso, 2000, 49–72; Christopher Hitchens, 'The Greater Evil', *The Nation*, 18 November 1996; Christopher Hitchens, 'Minority Report', *The Nation*, 14 November 1994; also, for a pithy summary of his indictment of the Clintons, see Christopher Hitchens, 'An Open Letter to Gore Vidal', *The Nation*, 2 November 1998.

44 See Christopher Hitchens, *No One Left to Lie To: The Values of the Worst Family*, London: Verso, 2000.

45 Christopher Hitchens, 'Thinking Like an Apparatchik', *The Atlantic*, July 2003.

46 Christopher Hitchens, 'Conspiracies with Sidney', *Nation*, 30 March 1998; Alexander Cockburn, 'Hitch the Snitch', *Counterpunch*, 15 June 1999.

47 Peter Carlson, 'Hitchens: Journalism's British Bad Boy', *Washington Post*, 12 February 1999.

48 Segments of this documentary can be seen on YouTube. 'Christopher Hitchens "Hitch Hike" Documentary', YouTube.com, 21 November 2011.

49 Ali, interview, 3 January 2012.

50 Christopher Hitchens, 'Gov. Death', *Salon*, 7 August 1999.

51 See, for example, Christopher Hitchens, 'Hardball with Chris Matthews', *MSNBC*, 30 November 2000; Christopher Hitchens, 'Dirty Rotten Scoundrels', *Observer*, 12 November 2000.

52 Christopher Hitchens, 'Cowboy', in *A Long Short War*.

53 Christopher Hitchens, 'No Regrets', *Slate*, 19 December 2009.

54 Christopher Hitchens, introduction to *Prepared for the Worst*, 4.

55 Christopher Hitchens, 'The Life of Johnson', in *For the Sake of Argument*;

Christopher Hitchens, 'The Cruiser', in *Unacknowledged Legislation*; Christopher Hitchens, 'Creon's Think-Tank: The Mind of Conor Cruise O'Brien', in *Prepared for the Worst*.

56   Christopher Hitchens, 'Hawks in the Dovecote', *Observer*, 25 August 2002.

57   Stephen Marshall, 'The Last Revolution in Town', *3am Magazine*, 29 May 2007.

58   Hitchens, *Hitch-22*, Kindle location 188–93.

59   Hitchens wrote: 'Has anybody resigned, from either the public or the private sectors (overlapping so lavishly as they now do)? Has anybody even offered to resign? Have you heard anybody in authority apologize, as in: "So very sorry about your savings and pensions and homes and college funds, and I feel personally rotten about it"? Have you even heard the question being posed? O.K., then, has anybody been fired? Any regulator, any supervisor, any runaway would-be golden-parachute artist? Anyone responsible for smugly putting the word "derivative" like a virus into the system?' Christopher Hitchens, 'America the Banana Republic', *Vanity Fair*, 9 October 2008. On Wisconsin see Christopher Hitchens, 'Don't Mess with Wisconsin', *Vanity Fair*, 28 February 2011.

60   Neil Munro, 'Leaving the Left', *National Journal,* April 5, 2003.

61   Christopher Hitchens, (2003) *Why Orwell Matters*, New York: Basic Books, Kindle location 2256–58. This discussion occurs in a chapter wherein the bold contrarian hazards to deconstruct the postmodernists. Alex Callinicos also recalls that Hitchens was not always an especially powerful analyst. He describes a review by Hitchens in the *New Statesman* of Perry Anderson's *Arguments Within English Marxism* which 'got everything wrong'.

62   On the Halliburton argument see Christopher Hitchens, 'Oleaginous', in *A Long Short War*. I am indebted to Dennis Perrin for pointing out this example.

63   Hitchens had early stipulated this distinction between monopoly capital and free enterprise: 'I still think that monopoly capitalism can and should be distinguished from the free market and that it has certain fatal tendencies in both the short and long term.' Christopher Hitchens, *Letters to a Young Contrarian*, New York: Perseus, 2001, 102.

2 ENGLISH QUESTIONS, FROM ORWELL TO THATCHER

1   Christopher Hitchens, 'Lessons Maggie Taught Me', *Nation*, 17 December 1990; Christopher Hitchens, 'The Misfortune of Poetry', *Atlantic*, October 2002; Christopher Hitchens, 'Credibility Brown', *London Review of Books*,

17 August 1989; Christopher Hitchens, *Hitch-22: A Memoir*, London: Allen & Unwin, 2011, Kindle location 3282.

2   Stuart Hall, 'Gramsci and Us', *Marxism Today*, June 1987.

3   Stuart Hall, 'The Great Moving Right Show', in Stuart Hall and Martin Jacques, eds., *The Politics of Thatcherism*, London: Lawrence & Wishart, 1983, 28–9.

4   Christopher Hitchens, 'Something about the Poems', in *Unacknowledged Legislation: Writers in the Public Sphere*, London: Verso, 2002, 249; Christopher Hitchens, 'Churchillian Delusions', *For the Sake of Argument: Essays and Minority Reports*, London: Verso, 1993, 84–6; Hitchens, *Hitch-22*, Kindle locations 3316, 3343–44.

5   Christopher Hitchens, 'Reactionary Cheek', *Nation*, 26 May 1979.

6   Christopher Hitchens, 'This Thatchered Land, This England', *Nation*, 19–26 July 1980.

7   Hitchens, 'Something about the Poems', 245; Christopher Hitchens, 'Lessons Maggie Taught Me'.

8   D. D. Guttenplan, interview by author, 10 May 2012.

9   Amy Wilentz, 'Christopher Hitchens: Why Did I Adore him?', *Los Angeles Times*, 1 January 2012.

10   Decca Aitkenhead, 'Christopher Hitchens: "I Was Right and They Were Wrong"', *Guardian*, 22 May 2010.

11   On the Argentinian planning for, and fall out from, the Falklands/Malvinas conflict, see Klaus Friedrich Veigel, *Dictatorship, Democracy, and Globalization: Argentina and the Cost of Paralysis, 1973–2001*, University Park: Pennsylvania State University Press, 2009.

12   Anthony Barnett, 'Iron Britannia', *New Left Review*, July–August 1982.

13   Christopher Hitchens, 'On Not Knowing the Half of It: Homage to Telegraphist Jacobs', in *Prepared for the Worst: Selected Essays and Minority Reports*, London: Chatto & Windus, 1988, 345.

14   See Paul Gilroy and Joe Simm, 'Law, Order and the State of the Left', *Capital and Class* 9: 1, spring 1985.

15   See Linda Colley, *Britons: Forging the Nation 1707-1837*, New Haven: Yale University Press, 3rd edition, 2009.

16   Hitchens, *Hitch-22*, Kindle location 767–68; Paul Gilroy, *After Empire: Melancholia or Convivial Culture?*, London: Routledge, 2004, 108.

17   Christopher Hitchens, 'Londonistan Calling', *Vanity Fair*, November 2007.

18   For an excellent guide to the British media's representations of Islam, see John E. Richardson, *(Mis)Representing Islam: The Racism and Rhetoric of British Broadsheet Newspapers*, Amsterdam: John Benjamins, 2004.

19   Hitchens, *Hitch-22*, Kindle locations 1754–57, 7165–67.

20 Paul Lauter, *Canons and Contexts*, Oxford: Oxford University Press, 1990, 156.

21 Hitchens, *Unacknowledged Legislation*, xiii.

22 Franco Moretti, *Atlas of the European Novel, 1800–1900*, London: Verso, 1999, 151–8. Aside from the imperialist dimension, the insularity of the English ruling classes in the nineteenth century partly followed from its decision to wage war on revolutionary France. For about two decades, landowners and industrialists used to traversing the continent and imbibing its literature and arts, were confined to their small island. See Claire Tomalin, *Shelley and His World*, London: Penguin 1992, 2.

23 Jonah Raskin, *The Mythology of Imperialism: A Revolutionary Critique of British Literature and Society in the Modern Age*, New York: Monthly Review Press, 2009, 46.

24 See Christopher Hitchens, 'A Sense of Mission: The Raj Quartet' and 'The Blood Never Dries' in *Prepared for the Worst*; Christopher Hitchens, 'Old Man Kipling', in *Unacknowledged Legislation*; Christopher Hitchens, 'The Bard of Empires', in *Blood, Class, and Nostalgia: Anglo-American Ironies*, New York: Farrar, Strauss & Giroux, 1990.

25 Christopher Hitchens, *Arguably*, London: Atlantic Books, 2011, Kindle location 377-9.

26 Hitchens, 'Old Man Kipling', 150.

27 Hitchens, 'Bard of Empires'; Christopher Hitchens, 'A Man of Permanent Contradictions', *Atlantic*, June 2002. For a critique of the notion of Anglophone succession, see Patrick O'Brien, 'The Myth of Anglophone Succession', *New Left Review*, November–December 2003.

28 Christopher Hitchens, 'Minority Report', *Nation*, 19 October 1992.

29 Hitchens, 'A Man of Permanent Contradictions'.

30 By far the two superior essays on Kipling are by Edward W. Said and Jonah Raskin. See chap. 2 of Jonah Raskin, in *The Mythology of Imperialism*, New York: Monthly Review Press, 2002; and Edward W. Said, *Culture and Imperialism*, New York: Vintage, 1994, 159–96.

31 Hitchens, 'A Man of Permanent Contradictions'.

32 Hitchens, 'Something about the Poems'; Philip Larkin, *Collected Poems*, London: Marvell Press, 2003, 133–4, 141.

33 Alexander Cockburn, 'St. George's List', *Nation*, 7 December 1998. For a compendium of the gravest charges against Orwell, coupled with a polemic against Hitchens, see Scott Lucas, *The Betrayal of Dissent: Beyond Orwell, Hitchens and the New American Century*, London: Pluto Press, 2004.

34 Christopher Hitchens, *Why Orwell Matters*, New York: Basic Books, 2003, Kindle location 1983. Also published as *Orwell's Victory*. See also John

Newsinger's much briefer but more nuanced defence of Orwell in *Orwell's Politics*, London: Palgrave Macmillan, 1999, 146–7. For a general outline of some of Orwell's shifting positions and contradictions, see Jonah Raskin, 'George Orwell and the Big Cannibal Critics', *Monthly Review*, May 1983.

35 Hitchens, *Why Orwell Matters*, Kindle locations 1847–48; Andrew N. Rubin and أندرو روبين, 'Orwell and Empire: Anti-Communism and the Globalization of Literature', *Alif: Journal of Comparative Poetics*, 28, 2008.

36 Hitchens, *Why Orwell Matters*, Kindle location 1926–27.

37 Ibid., 1239–42, 1952–53, 1957–58. Pedantically, and trivially, Hitchens pointed out that in his essay 'On the Components of National Culture', Perry Anderson had tabulated the national origin of major émigré intellectuals in the United Kingdom – thereby suggesting that such references could have benign and defensible purposes. Orwell's listing national, racial, and sexual details had no analytical value whatsoever. It was purely connotative, evoking that unreliability against which he was trying to guard.

38 Hitchens, *Why Orwell Matters*, Kindle location 908–909.

39 See Raymond Williams, '*Nineteen Eighty Four* in 1984', *Marxism Today*, January 1984; Hitchens, *Why Orwell Matters*, Kindle location 896–903. For an intelligent critique of Williams, see Dennis Donoghue, *England, Their England: Commentaries on English Language and Literature*, Berkeley: University of California Press, 1988, 319–22.

40 Hitchens, *Why Orwell Matters*, Kindle location 1502–57. See also George Orwell, 'The English People', in *The Collected Letters, Essays and Journalism of George Orwell: Vol. 3, As I Please*, New York: Penguin, 1971, 15–56; George Orwell, 'The Lion and the Unicorn: Socialism and the English Genius', 1941, republished at www.gutenberg.org; Newsinger, *Orwell's Politics*, 61–88.

41 Hitchens, *Why Orwell Matters*, Kindle location 1416–18.

42 George Orwell, 'As I Please', *Tribune*, 14 February 1947.

43 George Orwell, 'My Country Right or Left', 1940, republished at www.orwell.ru.

44 Hitchens, *Why Orwell Matters*, Kindle location 1505; George Orwell, 'The English People', in *Collected Letters*, 3:15–56; Orwell, 'Lion and the Unicorn';' Newsinger, *Orwell's Politics*, 61–88.

45 Orwell, 'English People', 15–56.

46 Orwell, 'Lion and the Unicorn'.

47 Perry Anderson wrote 'On the Components of National Culture' in 1968 in an attempt to arm a potential student movement with the rudiments of a critique of Britain's limited, parochial intellectual culture and the educational apparatuses that perpetuated it. Critical to his diagnosis was

that the dominant industrial bourgeoisie had never been compelled to elaborate a revolutionary Enlightenment critique of society; it had come to power through a process of arduous accommodation with the aristocratic capitalists who had previously dominated and had thus never had to remake society 'from scratch', as it were. The stability of the British ruling class – partially manifest in what Hitchens valued as the 'splendid and unique privilege of traceable, stable community' – was compounded by the fact that, unlike almost every major European society, it had not suffered occupation, conquest, civil war, or revolution by the time of the Second World War. The consequence was that it developed no body of totalising social thought comparable to that of Durkheim, Pareto, and Weber and instead tended to produce a set of isolated disciplines working on discrete problems within the social formation in the spirit of melioration. Had the British ruling class ever been faced with a working-class movement armed with the totalising thought of Marxism, as had, for example, the Prussian Junkers, it too would have had to retort with a Weber of its own. It was left to a radical wing of the intelligentsia to produce something like this – but the only radicalisation of the intelligentsia that occurred before the Second World War was a brief flux in the turmoil of the 1930s, and then its influence was largely on intellectuals in the field of letters or science, with neither able to sustain a lasting reconstruction of intellectual culture. Moreover, the influx of European intellectuals to British academic institutions after the war tended to be predominantly composed of 'White' exiles, conservatives, or liberals fleeing radical social change and at home in the staid traditionalism of British society. They thrived in a culture that had exhausted its own resources of ingenuity, precisely because of the vitiating effect of its parcellised nature, and in every major respect reinforced its narrowness, its prejudices, and its 'common sense'. Anderson's essay originally appeared in *New Left Review*, July–August 1968.

48 Hitchens, *Why Orwell Matters*, Kindle locations 1517, 1534; Orwell, 'English People' ; Orwell, 'Lion and the Unicorn';' Newsinger, *Orwell's Politics*, 61–88.

49 Christopher Hitchens, 'Where the Twain Should Have Met', *Atlantic*, September 2003; Christopher Hitchens, 'My Friend Edward', *The Observer*, 28 September 2003.

50 Hitchens, *Hitch-22*, Kindle locations 7279–80, 7329–30.

51 Ibid., 7182.

52 Ibid., 7376–79, 7388–89.

53 Ibid., 7390–91.

54 Hitchens, 'Where the Twain Should Have Met.'

55 Ibid.

56   Clare Brandabur, 'Hitchens Smears Edward Said', *Counterpunch*, 19–21 September 2003.

57   See Edward W. Said, *Orientalism*, New York: Penguin, 2003; Edward W. Said, *Covering Islam: How the Media and the Experts Determine How We See the Rest of the World*, New York: Vintage, 1997. For a useful summary of Said's ideas, see Bill Ashcroft and Pal Ahluwalia, *Edward Said*, London: Routledge, 1999. For a Marxist perspective on the concept of 'the West', see Silvia Federici, ed., *Enduring Western Civilization: The Construction of the Concept of Western Civilization and Its 'Others'*, Westport, CT: Praeger, 1995.

58   Many of Said's articles from his later years are available online at edwardsaid.org.

59   Hitchens, 'Where the Twain Should Have Met'.

60   Hitchens, *Hitch-22*, Kindle location 8381. Suffice to say Warraq's text – which accuses Said of 'intellectual terrorism', argues that he does not believe in the truth, and finds his use of terms such as *discourse* pretentious in an academic – is far from 'the best critique' of *Orientalism*. Ibn Warraq, *Defending the West: A Critique of Edward Said's 'Orientalism'*, Amherst: Prometheus Books, 2007.

61   See Aijaz Ahmad, 'Orientalism and After', in *In Theory: Classes, Nations, Literatures*, London: Verso, 2008.

62   Hitchens, 'Where the Twain Should Have Met'.

63   On Marx and India see Aijaz Ahmad, ed., *Karl Marx and Friedrich Engels: On the National and Colonial Questions: Selected Writings*, New Delhi: Leftword, 2001; Christopher Hitchens, 'A Sense of Mission: The Raj Quartet', *Grand Street*, winter 1985 Hitchens's stance was in some ways rather close to that of a slightly obscure Marxist theorist named Bill Warren, who sought to repudiate anti-imperialism. See Bill Warren, *Imperialism: Pioneer of Capitalism*, London: Verso, 1980.

64   Hitchens, *Hitch-22*, Kindle location 7393–95.

65   Adam Shatz, 'The Left and 9/11', *Nation*, 5 September 2002. Hitchens's brief description most closely resembles the London-based newspaper *Al-Hayat*, a platform for liberal Arab opinion for which Edward Said wrote regularly.

66   Guttenplan, interview; Tariq Ali, interview by author, 3 January 2012.

3 GUILTY AS SIN: THEOPHOBIA, FROM RUSHDIE TO THE WAR ON TERROR

1   Christopher Hitchens, *God Is Not Great: How Religion Poisons Everything*, 2012, Kindle location 107.

2   Ibid., 113.

3   Christopher Hitchens, *Hitch-22: A Memoir*, 2011, Kindle location 4944.

4   Ibid., 4980. See also Christopher Hitchens, 'Not Dead Yet', *Unacknowledged Legislation: Writers in the Public Sphere*, London: Verso, 2002, 126.

5   Christopher Hitchens, 'Siding with Rushdie', in *For the Sake of Argument: Essays and Minority Reports*, London: Verso, 1993, 297.

6   It is in this light that the refrain 'he knew what he was doing' – which induced Hitchens's remark that *of course* Rushdie knew what he was doing, since he was the author of the book – must be comprehended. Hitchens, 'Not Dead Yet', 126–7. On the cultural politics of the Rushdie affair, see Paul Gilroy, 'Frank Bruno or Salman Rushdie?', *Small Acts: Thoughts on the Politics of Black Cultures*, London: Serpent's Tail, 1993, 86–94.

7   Hitchens, *Hitch-22*, Kindle location 5024–27.

8   Christopher Hitchens, 'Salman Rushdie and *The Satanic Verses*', C-SPAN, 21 February 1989, c-spanvideo.org/program/Salm.

9   Christopher Hitchens, 'Minority Report', *Nation*, 13 March 1989.

10   Edward W. Said, *Covering Islam: How the Media and the Experts Determine How We See the Rest of the World*, New York: Vintage, 1997.

11   On the role of media representations in this, see Simon Cottle, 'Reporting the Rushdie Affair: A Case Study in the Orchestration of Public Opinion', *Race & Class* 32: 45, 1991.

12   Hitchens, *Hitch-22*, Kindle location 5014–19.

13   Hitchens, 'Not Dead Yet', 125–35.

14   Hitchens, 'Siding with Rushdie', 290.

15   Hitchens, *God Is Not Great*, Kindle location 2972–76.

16   Lesley Hazleton, 'Hazleton on Hitchens', *Accidental Theologist*, 3 February 2012; Terry Eagleton, *Reason, Faith and Revolution: Reflections on the God Debate*, New Haven, CT: Yale University Press, 2009, 6.

17   Christopher Hitchens, 'Better Off Without', in *Prepared for the Worst*, 146.

18   Eagleton, *Reason, Faith and Revolution*, 14.

19   Daniel C. Peterson, 'Editor's Introduction: God and Mr Hitchens', *FARMS Review* 19: 2, 2007, xi–xlvi. On the origin of the term *totalitarianism*, see Robert O Paxton, *The Anatomy of Fascism*, New York: Penguin, 2004, 211.

20   Eagleton, *Reason, Faith and Revolution*, 53.

21   Hitchens, *God Is Not Great*, Kindle location 3033–37.

22   Mary Midgley, *Wickedness: A Philosophical Essay*, London: Routledge, 1984, 208; Eagleton, *Reason, Faith and Revolution*, 24.

23   Hitchens, *God Is Not Great*, Kindle location 2976–77.

24   William J. Hamblin, 'The Most Misunderstood Book: Christopher Hitchens on the Bible', *FARMS Review* 21: 2, 2007, 47–95.

25   Ibid.

26   Christopher Hitchens, *The Portable Atheist: Essential Readings for the Nonbeliever*, 2007, Cambridge, MA: Da Capo, Kindle location 222.

27   Hitchens, *God Is Not Great*, Kindle locations 312–4, 322–3.

28   Quoted in Richard Dawkins, 'Illness Made Hitchens a Symbol of the Honesty and Dignity of Atheism', *Independent*, 17 December 2011.

29   Hitchens, *God Is Not Great*, Kindle location 336.

30   Tony Blair vs Christopher Hitchens, 'Religion Is a Force for Good in the World', sixth semiannual Munk Debate, Toronto, 26 November 2010, broadcast on C-SPAN, 25 December 2010.

31   For detail on this see Richard Seymour, *The Liberal Defence of Murder*, London: Verso, 2008, 226–8, 250–8.

32   Christopher Hitchens, 'Why Women Aren't Funny', *Vanity Fair*, January 2007; Christopher Hitchens, 'Viagra Falls', *Nation*, 25 May 1998; Christopher Hitchens, 'Minority Report', *Nation*, 24 April 1989; Hitchens, *God Is Not Great*, Kindle location 3195.

33   Christopher Hitchens, 'The Lord and the Intellectuals', *Harper's*, July 1982.

34   Hitchens, 'Better Off Without', 145–6.

35   Ibid., 146.

36   Martin Amis, 'The Age of Horrorism', *Observer*, 10 September 2006.

37   Hitchens, *Hitch-22*, Kindle location 5031–32.

38   Christopher Hitchens, 'Of Sin, the Left and Islamic Fascism', *Nation*, 24 September 2001.

39   Christopher Hitchens, Debate with Chris Hedges on 'Is God Great?', King Middle School, Berkeley, 24 May 2007

40   Boris Kachka, 'Are You There, God? It's Me, Hitchens', *New York Review of Books*, 26 April 2007.

41   For a useful discussion of this question, see John L. Esposito, 'Reformation or Revolution', in *The Oxford History of Islam*, Oxford: Oxford University Press, 1999.

42   Christopher Hitchens, 'Facing the Islamist Menace', *City Journal*, winter 2007; 'Is God Great?', debate by Christopher Hitchens and Chris Hedges, King Middle School, Berkeley, California, 24 May 2007. On suicide attacks, of both the religious and secular variety, see Robert Pape, *Dying to Win: The Strategic Logic of Suicide Terrorism*, New York: Random House, 2005; on Palestinian suicide attacks see Luca Ricolfi, 'Palestinians, 1981–2003', in D. Gambetta, ed., *Making Sense of Suicide Missions*, Oxford: Oxford University Press, 2005, 77–116. Farhad Khosrokavar, in his analysis of Muslim suicide attackers, emphasises as a crucial factor the 'humiliation experienced by Palestinians' that 'goes far beyond the symbolic order … Objective factors give the subjective feeling of humiliation an objective

substratum'. Farhad Khosrokavar, *Suicide Bombers: Allah's New Martyrs*, London: Pluto, 2005, 118.

43 Christopher Hitchens, 'The War Within Islam', *Slate*, 19 February 2007.

44 'Islamophobia: A Challenge for Us All', summary, Runnymede Foundation, 1997, runnymedetrust.org.

4 THE ENGLISHMAN ABROAD AND THE ROAD TO EMPIRE

1 Christopher Hitchens, *Hitch-22: A Memoir*, 2011, Kindle locations 3916–17, 3934.

2 Ibid., 3938; John Rose, interview by author, 12 May 2012; John Palmer, interview by author, 13 May 2012.

3 Hitchens, *Hitch-22*, Kindle location 3951–4080.

4 Christopher Hitchens, 'Minority Report', *Nation*, 19 October 1992.

5 David E. Stannard, 'Uniqueness as Denial: The Politics of Genocide Scholarship', in Alan S. Rosenbaum, ed., *Is the Holocaust Unique?: Perspectives on Comparative Genocide*, Boulder, CO: Westview, 2009, 298.

6 Richard Seymour, *The Liberal Defence of Murder*, London: Verso, 2012, 242.

7 Christopher Hitchens. *Hitch-22: A Memoir*, Allen & Unwin, 2011, Kindle location 4548.

8 Christopher Hitchens, 'Realpolitik in the Gulf: A Game Gone Tilt', in *For the Sake of Argument: Essays and Minority Reports*, London: Verso, 1993, 75–7; Christopher Hitchens, 'Churchillian Delusions', in *For the Sake of Argument*, 84–6; and Christopher Hitchens, 'Befriending the Kurds', in *For the Sake of Argument*, 91–3.

9 Christopher Hitchens, 'No End of a Lesson', in *For the Sake of Argument*, 87–9.

10 'Was the Gulf War a Just War?', debate by Christopher Hitchens and Morton Kondracke, 3 April 1991, Madison, Wisconsin, www.youtube.com.

11 Tariq Ali, interview by author, 3 January 2012.

12 'Christopher Hitchens and Others Debate Iraq on *Start the Week* 30 May 2005', excerpt of BBC programme posted online by Labour Friends of Iraq, 31 May 2005, labourfriendsofiraq.org.uk.

13 Dennis Perrin, 'Punchy', *Red State Son*, 2 June 2005.

14 By far the best and most balanced account of the Yugoslavian wars is Susan L. Woodward, *Balkan Tragedy: Chaos and Dissolution After the Cold War*, Washington, DC: Brookings Institution, 1995. Also see Susan L. Woodward, 'The Political Economy of Ethno-Nationalism in Yugoslavia', *Socialist Register*, Pontypool: Merlin Press, 2003. For a good critical account of the realpolitik of external actors, above all the United States, see David N. Gibbs, *First Do No Harm: Humanitarian Intervention*

and the Destruction of Yugoslavia, Nashville, TN: Vanderbilt University Press, 2009.

15   Christopher Hitchens, 'Minority Report', *Nation*, 15 March 1993.

16   Ibid., 7 June 1993.

17   Ibid., 30 May 1994.

18   Christopher Hitchens, 'In the Bright Autumn of My Senescence', *London Review of Books*, 6 January 1994.

19   Dennis Perrin, interview by author, 3 May 2012.

20   Christopher Hitchens, 'Bloody Blundering: Clinton's Cluelessness Is Selling Out Kosovo', *Salon*, 5 April 1999.

21   Christopher Hitchens, 'Ethnic Poisoning', *Nation*, 3 May 1999.

22   Christopher Hitchens, 'Srebrenica Revisited', *Nation*, 13 April 1999.

23   Clare Short, *Hansard*, 31 March 1999.

24   Hitchens, 'Ethnic Poisoning'.

25   My own view of the Balkan wars and the prowar liberals has been argued in Seymour, *Liberal Defence of Murder*, 190–216.

26   Christopher Hitchens, 'Genocide and the Bodybaggers', *Nation*, 29 November 1999.

27   'Hitchens: Clinton Could Sell Out Blair', BBC, 3 June 1999; Christopher Hitchens, 'Close, But No Cigar', *Nation*, 5 October 1998.

28   Alexander Cockburn, 'Kerrey, Scheer and Hitchens: Liberals Rush to Defend War Criminal', *Counterpunch*, 8 May 2001. For details of the massacre see G. Vistica, 'One Awful Night in Thanh Phong', *New York Times Magazine*, 25 April 2001.

29   J. Glazov, 'Frontpage Interview: Christopher Hitchens', *FrontPagemag.com*, 10 December 2003; Hitchens, *Hitch-22*, Kindle location 4604–14.

30   Christopher Hitchens, lecture at University of California, Berkeley, November 2002 www.youtube.com; Perrin, interview; Christopher Hitchens, 'We're Still Standing', *Evening Standard*, 12 September 2001; Christopher Hitchens, 'The Morning After', *Guardian*, 13 September 2001.

31   Christopher Hitchens, 'Of Sin, the Left and Islamic Fascism', *Nation*, 8 October 2001; 'Resurrecting Christopher Hitchens', blog entry by Sam Husseini at husseini.posterous.com, 31 December 2011.

32   Hitchens, *Hitch-22*, Kindle location 4578–79.

33   Mike Davis, 'The Flames of New York', *New Left Review*, November–December 2001; Christopher Hitchens, 'For Patriot Dreams', *Vanity Fair*, December 2001.

34   Christopher Hitchens, 'Ha Ha Ha to the Pacifists', *Guardian*, 14 November 2001.

35 Christopher Hitchens, *Letters to a Young Contrarian*, Oxford: Perseus, 2001, 99.

36 Christopher Hitchens, 'I Wanted It to Rain on Their Parade', *Mirror*, 18 February 2003.

37 On the *New Left Review* allegation, see Christopher Hitchens, 'Left-Leaving, Left-Leaning', *Los Angeles Times*, 16 November 2003, and Tariq Ali, 'Re-colonizing Iraq', *New Left Review*, May–June 2003. The only statement in the latter that Hitchens could possibly interpret in this way, with a great deal of contortion, was the following: 'The new President of South Korea, Roh Moo-hyun, elected with high hopes from the country's youth as an independent radical, disgraced himself instantly by offering not only approval of America's war in the Middle East, but troops to fight it, in the infamous tradition of the dictator Park Chung Hee in the Vietnam War. If this is to be the new Seoul, Pyongyang would do well to step up its military preparations against any repetition of the same adventure in the Korean peninsula.'

38 Christopher Hitchens, 'Murder by Any Other Name', *Slate*, 7 September 2004.

39 Naomi Klein, 'Bring Najaf to New York', *Nation*, 26 August 2004.

40 Naomi Klein, 'You Can't Bomb Beliefs', *Nation*, 30 September 2004.

41 Christopher Hitchens, 'Cindy Sheehan's Sinister Piffle', *Slate*, 15 August 2005; Christopher Hitchens, 'What Cindy Sheehan Really Wants', *Slate*, 19 August 2005; *Anderson Cooper 360 Degrees*, CNN, 15 August 2005; Alexander Cockburn, 'Hitch Backs Down: Says Sheehan Not a "Larouchie"!', *Counterpunch*, 24 August 2005; *Q&A with Brian Lamb*, C-SPAN, 26 April 2009.

42 Christopher Hitchens, 'Imperialism: Superpower Dominance, Malignant and Benign', *Slate*, 10 December 2002.

43 What Hitchens said was, 'I don't favor an invasion of Iraq. But I favor a confrontation with Saddam Hussein.' Edward W. Lempinen, 'How the Left Became Irrelevant', *Salon*, 29 October 2002; Quoted in 'Cakewalk', *Salon*, 28 March 2003; Christopher Hitchens, 'What Happens Next in Iraq', *Mirror*, 26 February 2003.

44 'A Discussion about Christopher Hitchens', *Charlie Rose*, 13 April 2012, charlierose.com.

45 Brian Reade, 'Two Out-of-control Despots', *Mirror*, 21 March 2003; Christopher Hitchens, 'Chew on This', *Stranger*, 16–22 January 2003; Christopher Hitchens, 'The War to Be Proud Of', *Weekly Standard* 10:47, 5–12 September 2005.

46 Christopher Hitchens, 'Powell Is Showing His Hand', *Mirror*, 5 February

2003; Christopher Hitchens, 'In Front of Your Nose', *Slate*, 25 October 2005; 'Powell Claims Iraq Is Harboring Al Qaeda Terrorists, But Leaves Out Evidence Implicating US Allies; We Hear Responses from Baghdad, France and Cameroon', *Democracy Now!*, 6 February 2003; Don Van Natta Jr., 'Portrait of a Terror Suspect: Is He the Qaeda Link to Iraq?' *International Herald Tribune*, 10 February 2003; Cam Simpson and Stevenson Swanson, 'Prisoner Casts Doubt on Iraq Tie to Al Qaeda', *Chicago Tribune*, 11 February 2003. For more on the al-Qaeda–Zarqawi disputes, see Jason Burke, *Al-Qaeda: The True Story of Radical Islam*, London: I. B. Tauris, 2004. For more on the Zarqawi myth see Loretta Napoleoni, *Insurgent Iraq: Al-Zarqawi and the New Generation*, New York: Seven Stories Press, 2005; and Nick Davies, *Flat Earth News*, London: Chatto & Windus, 2008.

47 Christopher Hitchens, *A Long Short War: The Postponed Liberation of Iraq*, New York: Plume, 2003, 60–2. Unfortunately: BBC, 'Iraq War "Increased Terror Threat"', 2 February 2004; Andrew Grice, 'Iraq War Increased the Threat of Attacks, Says Major', *Independent*, 26 July 2005; Bryan Bender, 'Study Cites Seeds of Terror in Iraq', *Boston Globe*, 17 July 2005.

48 Christopher Hitchens, "Nowhere to Go," *Slate*, 22 November 2005.

49 M. Ludders, 'Columnist Hitchens Lectures on Political Dissent', *Kenyon Collegian*, 18 November 2004; 'An Interview with Christopher Hitchens ("Moral and Political Collapse" of the Left in the US)', *Washington Prism*, 16 June 2005, washingtonprism.org. Available at: <http://www.freerepublic.com/focus/f-news/1457374/posts>

50 J. Laksin, 'Christening the David Horowitz Freedom Center', *Frontpagemag.com*, 14 September 2006; C. Hitchens, 'Facing the Islamist Menace', *Frontpagemag.com*, 14 September 2006.

51 Tariq Ali, interview by author, 3 January 2012.

52 Grace Moore, *Dickens and Empire: Discourses of Class, Race and Colonialism in the Works of Charles Dickens*, Aldershot: Ashgate, 2004, 94, 113 and 167.

53 Ian Parker, 'He Knew He Was Right', *New Yorker*, 16 October 2006.

54 Hitchens, *Hitch-22*, Kindle locations 5656–72, 5674, 5692.

55 Stephen Marshall, 'The Last Revolution in Town', *3am Magazine*, 29 May 2007, www.3ammagazine.com.

56 Hitchens, *Hitch-22*, Kindle locations 5686–87, 5760–62.

57 Alexander Cockburn, 'Israel's Deadly Siege of Palestine: Hitch Hails the "Glorious War"', *Counterpunch*, 27 June 2006.

58 Christopher Hitchens, '(Un)intended Consequences', in *A Long Short War*, 80; Christopher Hitchens, 'That Bleeding Heart Wolfowitz', *Slate*, 22 March 2005; Christopher Hitchens, 'Sliming Wolfowitz', *Slate*, 17 April 2007; Christopher Hitchens, 'A Brave Woman Scorned', *Slate*, 14 May 2007. On

Wolfowitz's career see Jack Davis, 'The Challenge of Managing Uncertainty: Paul Wolfowitz on Intelligence Policy-Relations', *Studies in Intelligence* 39: 5, 1996, 35–42; Tim Shorrock, 'Paul Wolfowitz, Reagan's Man in Indonesia, Is Back at the Pentagon', *Foreign Policy in Focus*, 1 February 2001.

59   Christopher Hitchens, 'Lay Off Chalabi', *Slate*, 24 April 2003; Christopher Hitchens, 'Ahmad and Me', *Slate*, 27 May 2004.

60   On Chalabi's life and times see Aram Roston, *The Man Who Pushed America to War: The Extraordinary Life, Adventures, and Obsessions of Ahmad Chalabi*, New York: Nation Books, 2008. The evidence presented in the book tends to undermine its main thesis that Chalabi pushed anyone to war, but it does show that Chalabi is an intelligent operator who took advantage of opportunities provided by the confluence of political developments in Washington, DC, and the networks of power and influence that he cultivated from early on.

61   Hitchens, *Hitch-22*, Kindle location 5972–73.

62   Christopher Hitchens, 'A Death in the Family', *Vanity Fair*, November 2007.

CONCLUSION: TWENTY-TWENTY BLINDFOLD

1   Iraq war debate by George Galloway and Christopher Hitchens at Baruch College, New York, hosted by Amy Goodman, 14 September 2005, C-SPAN Video Library; Christopher Hitchens, 'The Lancet's Slant: Epidemiology Meets Moral Idiocy', *Slate*, 16 October 2006; Christopher Hitchens, 'The Case for Regime Change', in Thomas Cushman, ed., *A Matter of Principle: Humanitarian Arguments for War*, Berkeley: University of California Press, 2005, 38.

2   Christopher Hitchens, 'Holiday in Iraq', *Vanity Fair*, February 2007.

3   Juan Cole, 'Kamal Sayid Qadir Jailed for Criticism of Barzani', *Informed Comment*, 29 March 2006.

4   Odisho Malko, 'No Votes in Ninevah', *Guardian*, 23 February 2005; Mardean Isaac, 'The Desperate Plight of Iraq's Assyrians and Other Minorities', *Guardian*, 24 December 2011; Dilip Hiro, 'The Sarajevo of Iraq: Worsening Kurdish-Arab Friction Threatens the Region', *TomDispatch*, 22 July 2004.

5   In fact, Ghannouchi represents one of the most pluralist and democratic Islamist currents in the world, and he was exiled because his party was the target of some bloody repression, particularly in the early 1990s. On An-Nahda see Francois Burgat and William Dowell, *The Islamic Movement in North Africa*, Austin: University of Texas Press, 1993; Linda G. Jones, 'Portrait of Rashid Al-Ghannoushi', *Middle East Report*, no. 153, July–August 1988. The fear of Islamist resurgence is still being used to justify potential restrictions on democracy in postrevolutionary Tunisia. See Rachel Linn,

'Tunisia Must Hold Its Nerve for Democracy's Sake', *Guardian*, 11 August 2011.

6   Christopher Hitchens, 'At the Desert's Edge', *Vanity Fair*, July 2007.

7   Christopher Hitchens, 'Tunisia, the Arab world's Most Civilized dictatorship', *National Post*, 18 January 2011.

8   Agence France-Presse, 'Iran Opposition Says 72 Killed in Vote Protests', 3 September 2009; 'Tunisia Protests Against Ben Ali Left 200 Dead, says UN', *BBC News*, 16 May 2009. While Ben Ali never achieved less than 90 per cent of the vote – a fact Hitchens acknowledged made him nervous – Ahmadinejad's arguably rigged election result in 2009, with his campaign claiming 62 per cent of the vote, was not typical of Iranian elections. Further, US officials maintain that Ahmadinejad's fraud exaggerated his victory and that he would have won without it. See Christopher Dickey, 'The Supreme Leader', *The Daily Beast*, 19 July 2009.

9   For background on the origins of the Ben Ali dictatorship, its repression, and neoliberal policies, see Clement Henry Moore, 'Tunisia and Bourguibisme: Twenty Years of Crisis', *Third World Quarterly* 10: 1, January 1988; Karen Pfeifer, 'How Tunisia, Morocco, Jordan and Even Egypt Became IMF "Success Stories" in the 1990s', *Middle East Report*, 210, spring 1999; L. B. Ware, 'The Role of the Tunisian Military in the Post-Bourguiba Era', *Middle East Journal* 39: 1, winter 1985; Christopher Alexander, 'Authoritarianism and Civil Society in Tunisia', *Middle East Report* 205, 1997; Christopher Alexander, 'Tunisia's Protest Wave: Where It Comes from and What It Means', *Foreign Policy*, 3 January 2011.

10   Christopher Hitchens, 'What I Don't See at the Revolution', *Vanity Fair*, April 2011.

11   Christopher Hitchens, 'Egypt: Islamism Meets Realism', Council for Secular Humanism, n.d., secularhumanism.org.

12   Christopher Hitchens, 'The Iraq Effect', *Slate*, 28 March 2011.

13   *World Affairs Journal*; 'Drinking with Christopher Hitchens and the Iraqis', blog entry by Michael J. Totten, 6 February 2005.

14   Christopher Hitchens, 'The Iraq Effect', *Slate*, 28 March 2011. Hitchens also credited the stout diligence of Scottish justice in hunting down the alleged Libyan suspects in the Lockerbie attack but neglected to mention that Gadhafi had handed over the pair in 1999, as part of his nuptials with the European Union – long before the American mailed fist smashed into Baghdad.

15   Ronald Bruce St John, '"Libya Is Not Iraq": Preemptive Strikes, WMD and Diplomacy', *Middle East Journal* 58: 3, summer 2004. Mohammed El Baradei, who headed the International Atomic Energy Authority, said at

the time that 'Libya's nuclear weapons program was embryonic and its scientists were far from producing a weapon.' *Los Angeles Times*, 'Nuclear Inspectors Tour 4 Libyan Sites', 29 December 2003.

16   As far as I was able to discover in his published works and with the use of LexisNexis, he had barely mentioned Libya before the war on terror except to note the Reagan bombing campaign in 1986. Even during the war on terror, Hitchens devoted no single article to the country and generally mentioned it only in passing to gloat over Bush's triumph in forcing Gadhafi to disarm.

17   Christopher Hitchens, 'Is Barack Obama Secretly Swiss?', *Slate*, 25 February 2011. See also Christopher Hitchens, 'Don't Let Qaddafi Win', *Slate*, 14 March 2011.

18   *World Affairs Journal*; 'An Interview with Christopher Hitchens, Part II', blog entry by Michael J. Totten, 12 January 2010.

19   Christopher Hitchens, 'American Inaction Favors Qaddafi', *Slate*, 7 March 2011.

20   Hitchens to Tucker Carlson on *CNN Crossfire*, quoted in Marc Mulholland, *Daily Moiders*, 6 July 2004. (Website now defunct).

21   Xeni Jardin, 'Al-Cajun? Army Times Calls NOLA Katrina Victims "the Insurgency"', *Boing Boing*, 3 September 2005, boingboing.net; *Democracy Now*, 'George Galloway vs. Christopher Hitchens on the Bush Administration Response to Hurricane Katrina', 16 September 2005, www.democracynow.org.

22   Christopher Hitchens, 'America the Banana Republic', *Vanity Fair*, 9 October 2008.